GREEK

SCULPTURE

GREEK

TEXT BY PIERRE DEVAMBEZ

CURATOR, LOUVRE MUSEUM

PHOTOGRAPHS BY

ROBERT DESCHARNES

SELECTED AND ARRANGED BY

SONJA KNAPP AND JEAN IMBERT

SCULPTURE

TUDOR PUBLISHING COMPANY
NEW YORK

To modern eyes sculpture would appear to be the form of art on which the Greeks lavished their greatest care and enthusiasm. Such a judgment does not perhaps take due account of architecture nor, more especially, of painting which seems to have been even more greatly admired; perhaps we should think quite differently if the paintings and frescoes of Polygnotus, Zeuxis and Apelles had come down to us. It is because the sculpture of the Greeks is better known to us that we are inclined to assume that this was their favorite art form.

And yet our knowledge of it is far from complete. The passing of time has had its effect, and of all the great sculptors mentioned by the writers of antiquity, hardly any original work has survived. The names of Myron, Polycleitus and Lysippus would mean nothing to us were it not for the fact that, as early as the second century B.C., the great men of the time, capitalists and directors of academies, had had reproduced in great numbers, either for love of art, to decorate their palaces and villas, or to instruct their pupils in the craft, those statues which, to their mind, set the canons of beauty. Of these copies, some few have come down to us, of unequal merit and also, in many cases, differing one from another in a single movement or detail. In reproducing a model, the copyists did not feel themselves bound to a slavish exactitude.

Most of these copies were made from works of an art that was already mature and, in some cases, even sinking into decadence. The original works that we possess date, for the most part, from periods that were held in less esteem under the academism prevailing at the end of Antiquity. The excavations that have been carried out for almost a century now in Greece, Southern Italy, Sicily and the eastern part of the Mediterranean basin have fortunately brought to light sculptures far more ancient; their archaism having even by the fifth century passed out of favour, they had been ritually interred, or, more prosaically, quite simply thrown out as rubbish.

We are thus in possession of an almost unbroken series of sculptures in the round, either originals or copies, which take us from the beginning of the archaic period right through to the decadence.

Of the bas-reliefs, either decorating the walls of sacred or, more rarely, civic buildings, or else standing alone in the form of commemorative steles, copies were less often made, but they eventually suffered the same fate as the architectural whole to which they belonged, for which reason a great number of them have come down to us. Cemeteries and ruined temples have very often brought to light, sometimes almost in their original completeness, a whole decorative scheme which enables us to grasp the very conception and technique of those who created and executed it. It is quite certain that Phidias did not sculpture the Parthenon friezes with his own hand, and

yet it was under his direction that se
these give us a direct insight into

We do not propose to commer
tracing in broad outline the develo
a response in each one of us, wh

It must first be borne in mind
widely held, the general tendency
marble. The quarries of Pentele
shores of the Sea of Marmora or ir
centuries had passed during which
any artists, however outstanding,

There is however a single exc

4 · HARVEST PROCESSION (RELIEF ON A STEATITE VASE). HAGIA TRIADA (CRETE). 17TH CENTURY. ARCHAEOLOGICAL MUSEUM. IRAKLION. CRETE

third millenium B.C. and, in an excessively schematised form, represent the human, and especially the female, figure in a standing position generally, with the arms folded across the breast, the body flattened out and very thin — in fact so completely reduced to their magical significance as to entail the suppression of all those features not directly relevant to the magically functional idea of reproduction and fertility. The sex and the breasts are strongly marked, but in some cases the legs are not even indicated and the body, thus resembling the form of a violin, terminates in a curve more or less following the line of the groin and upper thigh. From a technical point of view, these idols are perfect. Fashioned in the neighbourhood of Paros, in carefully selected marble, lovingly polished by rubbing with emery powder, they appear primitive to us only by reason of their simplicity and suppression of detail, but the manner of their fashioning presupposes centuries of patient practice and experiment.

It is curious to note that the production of these idols did not survive the establishment of Crete's spiritual hegemony in the Mediterranean. Neither in the great island of Minos, nor later in the Mycenaean world did sculpture, at least of large-sized figures, find popular favour. The savage, lean-flanked lionesses overlooking the entrance to the palace at Mycenae appear to be such isolated examples in the art of the time that there is some justification for wondering whether they were not set up there, on either side of a symbolic column above the Main Gate, by strangers from Asia. It was not until their first contact with Egypt and the East, after the great Dorian invasion which put an end to Mycenaean civilization, that the Greeks really began to sculpture, not at first in marble but in a softer stone, a fairly common chalky stone called poros, the like of which may be found in many regions where no taste for sculpture ever developed as among the Greeks.

It was not, therefore, the marble that one stumbles across in so many parts of Greece, which gave the Hellenes their love of plastic art.

We are often inclined to overlook the fact that the greatest masterpieces admired by the Ancients were in bronze. Myron's Discobolus, Polycleitus' Diadumene and the statues of Lysippus were in this material, as well as many other works of lesser known artists. But in times when metal is scarce, bronze is at a premium, and even before the Middle Ages most of the statues in bronze which adorned public squares and sanctuaries had been melted down to become arms or tools. Whenever we see in a museum a marble figure leaning in a more or less arbitrary fashion on some artificial support, such as a tree trunk which appears quite out of place, we may be sure that we are looking at the copy of a bronze original which, owing to the ductility of this material, had been able to retain its balance without the aid of any adventitious support.

Work in bronze had begun long before the period of the great masters. It appears, in fact, that bronze was one of the favorite materials of those who first attempted plastic art, at least in regard to small-sized figures. For the technique of working bronze is very similar to that of working in clay, and it was in earth, in all probability, that men first modelled figures. It would be out of place here to go into technical details; let it suffice to recall that, like all the arts but perhaps even more than any other, sculpture is essentially dependent on its material, and that an artist cannot attempt to express himself unless he is first a master of his craft.

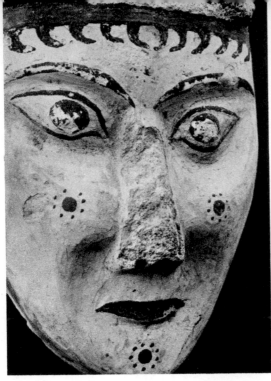

The similarity of technique in the working of clay and bronze explains why, in the beginning at least, statuettes were very small in size. It is awkward to model a large-sized figure in clay and even more difficult, once it is modelled, to avoid its cracking in the process of firing.

Earth and bronze are consequently the materials of most of the figurines that have come down to us from the Cretan and Mycenaean civilizations, and it was these materials that the Greeks first used when, after the Homeric period, they felt the need to dedicate as votive offerings in the sanctuaries those figures of oxen and horses which reproduced in miniature the outward aspect of the animals whose increase they desired, by the grace of heaven, in

7 · TATTOOED HEAD (PAINTED STUCCO). MYCENAE. 13TH CENTURY. NATIONAL MUSEUM. ATHENS

8 · GODDESS WITH SERPENT (FAIENCE). PALACE OF KNOSSOS (CRETE) 17TH CENTURY. ARCHAEOLOGICAL MUSEUM, IRAKLION.

9 · GRIFFIN'S HEAD (BRONZE) : DECORATING A CALDRON. 1ST HALF OF 7TH CENTURY. OLYMPIA MUSEUM

their own fields.

But Greek sculptors also delighted to work in less common materials. They carved statues in precious woods, such as cedar from Tyre, in ivory imported from Egypt and the East, and in gold mined on the very confines of the Greek world; and the combined technique known as chryselephantine was, at least for small-sized figures, one of the most popular at the dawn of the archaic period. Though abandoned in less prosperous times or when exchanges with the East had been interrupted for political reasons, these luxury techniques came into favour again during the classical period in the fifth century, and it was on a gigantic scale that Phidias, imitated by several of his contemporaries, carved in gold and ivory the statue of Zeus dedicated at Olympia, and the Athena that stood in the centre of the Parthenon.

The very diversity of these techniques practised by the Greeks is indicative of their love of plastic art: terra cotta, bronze, common stone, marble, and precious materials — their sculptors used them all. Now as we have seen, this taste for sculpture arose only after the Homeric period. It has been noted that the few passages in the Iliad and the Odyssey in which statues are mentioned do not belong to the text in its earliest form. The problem, therefore, is to find out how this taste first arose, and why it developed so suddenly and extensively.

At the present time we know next to nothing of Creto-Mycenaean mythology. It would seem, however, to have been far less rich, far less prolific in incident, than that which was later known to Homer. Admittedly we find on Minoan seals a goddess sitting under a tree receiving the homage of her devotees, but it is a ritual scene in which no action takes place, and the goddess herself took on distinguishable form only in statuettes in the round of rather diminutive size.

For the Greeks, on the other hand, their deities were more substantial. Those described in the Iliad and the Odyssey are so familiar to us that we feel no surprise at all when we find them coming down to earth to take part in a battle or to guide Ulysses to Alcinous' palace. It was this personality which Homer, and no doubt many other poets of the same period, had been able to give to these insubstantial beings, which caught the imagination of the people, and it was for this reason that it became necessary to place behind the altar, from which rose the smoke of the sacrifices offered to them, images reproducing as closely as possible the appearance of the god. In the second century A.D. the writer Pausanias could still speak of these rough stones, supposedly fallen from the skies, which in earliest times had been the divinity itself. How was it possible then that the Greeks, steeped as they were in a living literature in which Apollo, Zeus and Athena figured as distinct individuals, should continue to look upon these personages, who shared in their daily life, as reduced to the state of sacred stones, formless stones which nevertheless were clothed in wrappings and offered beasts for food and wine and milk to drink?

It was not enough, however, to conceive the idea that these sacred stones did not correspond to what might be expected: it still remained to find the means of fashioning an image that would give these gods the likeness suggested in the poetic descriptions. Until well into the seventh century the skill of the artists seems to have been unequal to the task. They were able, of course, to fashion small statuettes representing animals or even human figures, but it was quite another matter to carve stone statues which, in order to be convincing, had to be life-size, to remain upright, and to present more or less the correct proportions of the human body. For, and this is the essential point, Greek mythology is fundamentally anthropomorphic: the gods made man in their own image, and it was by representing the highest type of human beauty that the Greeks felt they were coming closest to the true aspect of the gods.

In order to create statues representing the Immortals, Greek sculptors had to follow models from other lands. In Egypt and in the East, experienced artists had for centuries produced effigies of their gods, their kings and their local dignatories. It was at the time when relations were first

established between Greece and Syria and the Nile Valley that sculptured images of great size first appeared on Hellenic soil.

As we have seen, the primary purpose of these images was to personify superhuman beings on whose goodwill the destiny of man was dependent. But almost contemporaneously, all those whose means permitted desired to place their own effigy before the eyes of the Immortals, and their images in stone were set up near the cult statue in the temple itself or in the sanctuary. Nor was this all: the dead were supposed to be in some way divine; they were in any case above the mass of humankind, and that is why statues representing the dead were often placed on tombs.

Votive offerings placed in sanctuaries were often made in gratitude for a favour granted by the god. Now the religious sentiment of the age could not envisage any happy event occuring otherwise than by the will of the gods. If a victory were won, homage was straightway paid to the gods, and with the growing popularity of athletic contests, of which the Olympic Games were the most famous, statues of athletes appeared in ever increasing numbers. We shall see further on that it was in large part due to these athletic votive offerings that movement was first introduced into plastic art, for in order that the offering be quite clear, it was necessary to reproduce the characteristic attitude of the victor, so that the discus-thrower could be distinguished at a glance from the wrestler, and from then

11 · 12 · KORE KNOWN AS "LADY OF AUXERR
(LIMESTONE). END OF 7TH CENTURY. LOUVRE MUSEUM. PA

13 · FEMALE FIGURE, DETAIL (LIMESTONE). ACROPOLIS
MYCENAE. 7TH CENTURY. NATIONAL MUSEUM. ATHE

14 · HERA (LIMESTONE). EARLY 6TH CENTURY. OLYMPIA MUSE

on there was no longer any question of modelling immobile figures, as in earlier times, in the mute receptive attitude suitable to deity in the presence of worshippers, as to mortal men standing to attention before their masters.

Such was the role of sculpture in the round, but sculpture in relief was no less important. If the temple was but a house, the god's house, a sense of fitness at least required that it should be distinguished from the dwellings of mere mortals. It was but natural that above the façade, in the triangular area formed by the epistyle and the sloping sides of the roof — an empty space known as the pediment — a scene should be depicted. It could, of course, be painted, and undoubtedly in the most ancient buildings made of sun-dried brick over a wooden framework, it was often deemed sufficient to paint in a scene. But in the bright sunlight of Greece, how much more effective it was to make the figures stand out in relief, thus benefiting from the play of light and shade. This is not to say, however, that color was entirely abandoned, for the Greeks, like all early peoples, practised only polychrome sculpture.

The pediment was not the only part of the building worthy of decoration. At the top of the building, above the colonnade, either Doric or Ionic, ran a space known as the frieze. There was no compelling reason for filling in these bands which were either unbroken or else cut across by the three vertical grooves of the triglyphs. But the desire to embellish the house of the god was, in the Greeks, allied to that passionate love of story which first appears so strikingly in the Homeric poems. The Greeks eagerly filled in every available space with a picture recalling some tale.

For while sculpture in the round, by its very nature, does not lend itself to narrative, sculpture in relief is, like line drawing, particularly adapted to the telling of a story or to illustrating some adventure.

There is no lack of story or adventure in Greek mythology. The gods, human in physical appearance, are human too in character, and in their passions. Zeus is continually falling in love with a mortal woman; Hera is jealous; Apollo must expiate by purification the murder of Pytho; while the story of the epic heroes is rich in incident. There was no lack of subject matter.

The Greeks by no means exhausted the repertoire at their disposal. There are legends known to us through literature, and heroes of considerable fame, that apparently never appealed to sculptors. Though illustrated in vase-painting, the adventures of Ulysses or Agamemnon never figured in relief, the reason being that sculpture, intended as it was for religious purposes, could treat only sacred subjects. Even among the divinities themselves, while some of them such as Athena, Zeus and Apollo had a widespread popularity and were venerated throughout the whole of Greece, others, such as Ares, seem to have inspired decorative artists only rarely; their story, moreover, was lacking in drama, and their cult not among the most flourishing. Furthermore, alongside the Pan-Hellenic heroes were other figures of purely local fame; Telephus, for instance, though honoured at Tegea where his story was treated by Scopas, was in other parts of the Hellenic world much less renowned.

In accordance with the order adopted, which was dependent on the nature of the building and the temperament of the artist, the figures continue in an unbroken line right round the building — this in an Ionic work — or else they are strictly enclosed in the narrow space of the metope; we can see here the contrast between the easy-going people of the East on the borders of Anatolia, and the more sober logic of the Dorian peoples. The former manner recalls the lengthy tales of Homer and Herodotus, the latter gives us an early indication of that love of drama which Aeschylus, Sophocles and Euripides portrayed so brilliantly on the stage of fifth-century Athens.

It would appear only reasonable that on sacred buildings, which for a long time were the only buildings thus decorated with sculpture, the themes chosen should be solely of a religious character. And this was in fact the case from about the middle of the sixth century B.C. But it seems difficult

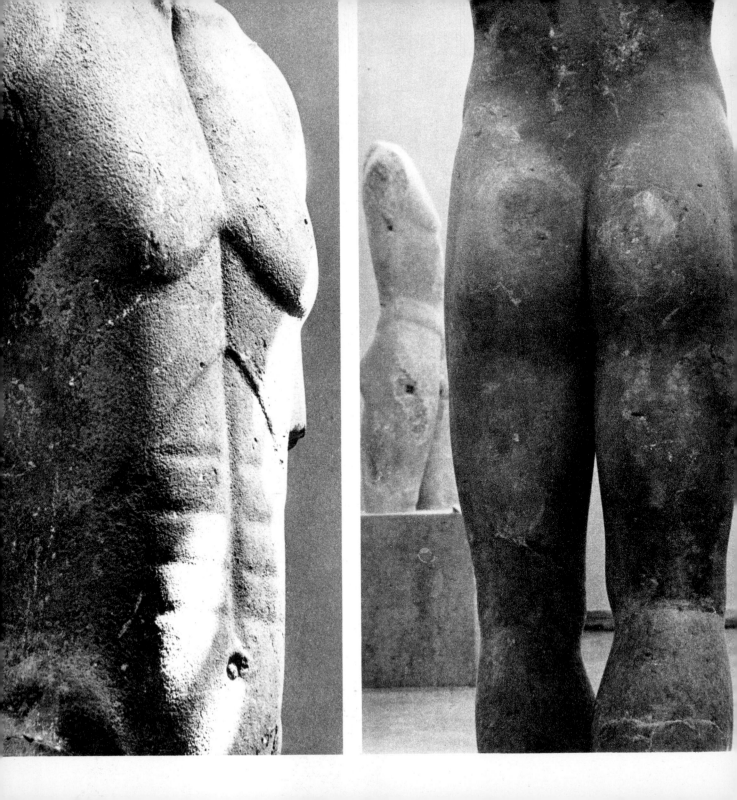

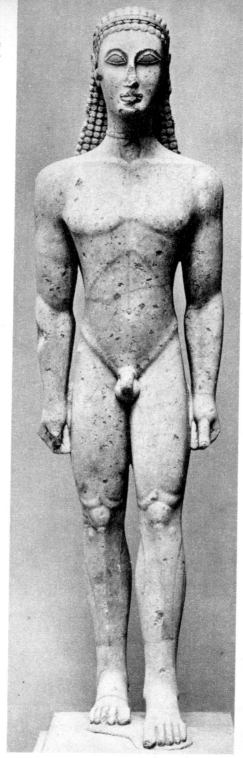

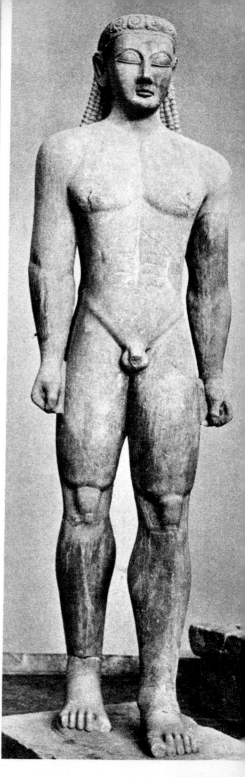

16 · TORSO OF GIGANTIC KOUROS (MARBLE). SET UP IN FRONT OF THE TEMPLE OF POSEIDON AT SOUNION. 600/590. NATIONAL MUSEUM. ATHENS

17 · BACK VIEW, KOUROS OF CEOS (MARBLE). NATIONAL MUSEUM. ATHENS

18 · KOUROS (MARBLE). ATTICA. 615/600. METROPOLITAN ART MUSEUM. NEW YORK

19 · GIGANTIC KOUROS (MARBLE). CAPE SOUNION. ATTICA. EARLY 6TH CENTURY. NATIONAL MUSEUM. ATHENS

to attribute any edifying or ritual significance to the scenes depicted on pediments or friezes in earlier times; the very variety of the themes and the juxtaposition of tales having no connection one with another lead us to assume that the main objective was to make the god's house a beautiful one, richer than all others, with decorative scenes pleasing to the eyes of mortal man as much as to the eyes of its divine occupant.

Thus sculpture in the round and sculpture in relief both held a place of great importance in the religious life of the Greeks, and as religion played a greater part in the life of the people of that time than in our modern world, since nothing took place without counsel being taken of the gods or thanks rendered to them, the demand for sculptors was sufficient to keep in employment a large number of workers.

Let us now consider what sort of men these sculptors were, and how they were recruited. Much has been made of the fact that in the Greek language the same word does duty for both art and technique, which has led to the conclusion that sculptors were little more than workmen, almost manual labourers, who were held in small esteem and whose work was practically anonymous. It is not impossible that this was so in earliest times. Yet it is hard to believe that the city which expended such vast sums of money on the construction of a temple in honour of its god should treat the person entrusted with the task of sculpturing the statue or decorating the pediment as a mere hired labourer whose sole task was to carry out the work allotted to him. If, from the whole archaic period, very few names of sculptors have come down to us, this is due not so much to the obscurity of these artists in their own lifetime as to the disfavour into which the primitives had fallen at the time of the classical period; almost all their works were then lost, and yet a few great names, in some cases legendary, still lingered on in the memory of men. Daedalus, supposedly responsible for so many inventions, was also held to have been a sculptor; even if he never existed, some of his presumed descendants were at least real persons, whose signatures were still extant at the time of Pausanias.

From the sixth century, we may mention Bathycles of Magnesia, whose skill took him from Asia Minor to Sparta to construct and decorate, in the neighborhood of the city, a vast monument decorated with sculpture, incorrectly known as the "throne of Amyclae."

Even before the beginning of the classical period, there were sculptors of great repute who attracted clients and disciples in great numbers. Ageledas had been, it was said, the master of Myron, Phidias and Polycleitus — only a legend, no doubt, but at least it proves that certain great masters were widely known. At a later date, Plato allowed Polycrates the honour of figuring in a dialogue with Socrates. As we all know, Phidias was not only a sculptor, but the real Director of Fine Arts in Periclean Athens, and in the fourth century, while Praxiteles seems to have belonged to what we should call the high society of his day, Lysippus was one of the favorite companions of Alexander of Macedon. If, therefore, it must be admitted that the sculptor's place in society was, in earliest times, a somewhat humble one, yet it was not very long before his role was such

that we should be justified in comparing the high esteem in which the great masters were held with that enjoyed by Matisse, Bourdelle and Rouault in our own century. And this was a fact of no small importance, for the prospect of success is always attractive, and it may be assumed that many a sculptor, who might otherwise never have realized his vocation, was spurred on to take up a career in art by the hope of achieving a fame equal to that of the fashionable artists of his day.

We have no certain knowledge of the financial demands of these sculptors. It may be supposed that for a long time — and this in itself proves that they were not from the lower social classes — the best of them made a point of receiving no "salary" for the works they executed. We know that a painter, Polygnotus, had asked no remuneration for the works he was engaged to do in one of the porticos of Athens. But this disdain of financial reward had won for him the honorary citizenship of Athens, and we may well imagine that those who, on the other hand, asked for financial reward were all the more exacting in that they considered their work beyond price. We have records of other painters at the end of the fifth century which prove to us that some of them were literally rolling in wealth.

It was, moreover, only at a very late date that clients, at least for large-scale works, were private individuals. Down as far as the fourth century at any rate, it was the local bodies, civic or religious, that engaged sculptors to carry out a group of statuary or a bas-relief. Nor should this surprise us, for we have already remarked on the omnipresence of the gods. Monuments were dedicated only in sanctuaries, and even the statues of athletes

21 · QUADRIGA. TERRA COTTA FROM BOEOTIAN TOMB. 1ST HALF OF 6TH CENTURY. NATIONAL MUSEUM. ATHENS

were no doubt erected at public expense, for a champion's victory redounded to the honor of the whole city, which claimed the glory as its own. Nor can we count as exceptional even such monuments as that to which the famous Charioteer of Delphi belonged, which was dedicated by a tyrant of Sicily, for tyrants, even though their power had no legal foundation, considered themselves as representing the states over which they ruled.

It was not until the time when individualism was rife, when the desire for a more comfortable life led to the more luxurious embellishment of the formerly simple homes of the Greeks, and particularly when, in the kingdoms that sprang up from the ruins of Alexander's empire, the newly-rich sought do dazzle their contemporaries with an ostentatious display of luxury, that the sculptors' clientele was mainly composed of private individuals. Every man was eager to have his portrait done in marble, and we may see side by side, in a house at Delos belonging to the second century B.C., the statues of the owner and his wife. Everyone was anxious to have in at least one room of his house, for his own delight and for that of his guests, a sort of little museum.

Let us now consider the external conditions under which Greek sculpture developed. From its beginnings during the seventh century right through to its decline at the time when the Romans had long since established their empire over the whole Mediterranean basin, Greek sculpture retains a certain number of fixed characteristics which constitute its particular originality.

The most striking of them, its tendency to generalize, is to be found also in all other manifest-ations of Hellenism. There are races who are interested only in the anecdotic, the episodic, the most fleeting aspects of life. The Greeks, on the other hand, in a way that was both unconscious and yet systematic, set themselves to see in personalities and in the stories in which they figured, only what was of lasting import, what was valid for life in general — life, that is to say, mankind, for to the Greeks nothing was of interest that did not directly concern man himself. They had no interest in natural landscape, nor in the animal kingdom, for these are not logical, nor subject to reason: they cannot think. Man on the contrary, in his most perfect form, that of the gods, is not only a marvel of physical harmony and proportion ; he is above all a thinking being who, consequently, can create ideas. A model is an end in itself: every ephemeral aspect of a man's body, his facial features and even his thoughts must be set aside, effaced as misleading. Whether this idea is to be found clearly expressed in ancient texts, I am not sure, but it stands out clearly when we come to examine ancient art, and especially sculpture.

Right from the beginning, when a human figure was to be represented, when a man or women of however striking physical appearance, dedicated their image to a divinity in a sanctuary, neither the client nor the artist was concerned that the most typical features of the model be reproduced. The man, even if he has passed the age for active sport and has never taken part in any contest, is always presented nude as an athlete in training, which in itself sets him apart from daily life. The woman is distinguished from other women only by her costume, which is always rich and beau-tiful. But the attitude is the same: the face is not clearly characterized, and when excavation brings to light an archaic statue of this kind, it is often very difficult to tell whether it represents

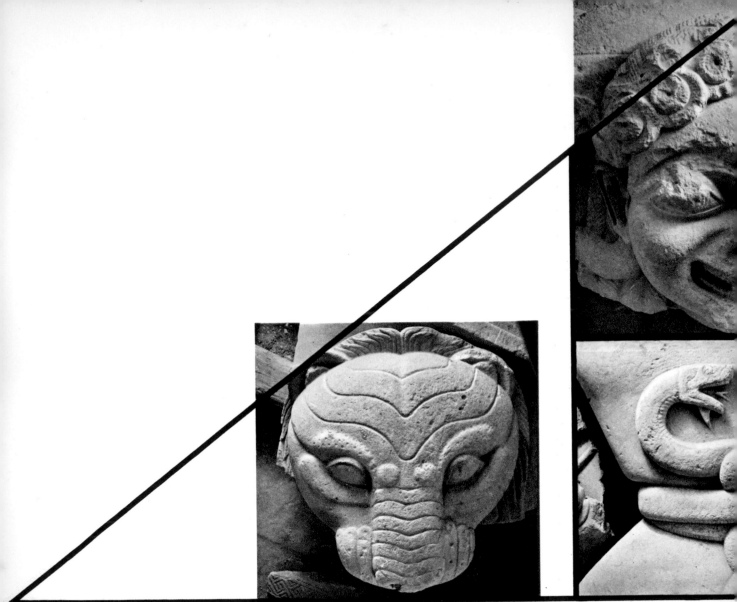

DETAILS OF PEDIMENT OF THE TEMPLE OF ARTEMIS (LIMESTONE). 1ST QUARTER O

ENTURY. ROYAL PALACE MUSEUM. CORFU

23 · HEAD OF PANTHER

24 · GORGON

25 · GORGON'S BELT

26 · HEAD OF CHRYSAOR

a human being or a divinity. Was this due to the inexperience of the artist, who was unable to pick out the typical features of his model? Assuredly not. Firstly, because the general tendency of primitive art was to accentuate the distinguishing features of the person whose likeness was to be reproduced, and secondly because, even in the classical period, at a time when technical difficulties raised no further problems for artists, we find the same concern for impersonality. Let us take, for example, that portrait of Pericles sculptured by Cresilas during the great states-man's lifetime, or at least within a few months of his death. It has often been pointed out that this is a typical portrait of the statesman as such, rather than of a particular man grown old in political strife and weighed down with worldly cares. Even after the fourth century, when the por-traits then appearing in great numbers took on a more realistic appearance, it can still be noted that the artist strives to suppress any features of his model that might seem too markedly indiv-idual.

In considering scenes figured in relief, we do not find, as in Eastern Art, occasional scenes or battle scenes, with warriors who had won fame in real combat. On the contrary, Greek reliefs are allusive rather than historical, and if we frequently come across friezes of Amazons in battle or scenes from the legendary Trojan War, it is because they would suggest to the beholder similar circumstances that he himself had witnessed. The Amazons and the Trojans symbolized, about 480 B.C., the Persians whose army had just been defeated at Marathon and Salamis. When we find on pediments at Olympia the Lapithae vigorously defending themselves against the impious advances of the Centaurs, it is because they represent, like the Greeks themselves, civilization triumphant over barbarism. In this respect, it would seem that sculpture lagged behind painting, for even in the middle of the fifth century a painting could be seen on the walls of the Portico known as the Poecile, representing, in a very realistic manner, the battle of Marathon. It was not till thirty or more years later that an episode taken from a real battle against the Persians was insin-uated hesitantly into the frieze surmounting the temple of the Athena Nike on the Acropolis.

Mention must also be made of the funerary steles, of which a great many were sculptured in Attica from the end of the fifth to the end of the fourth centuries B.C. The names of the dead are inscribed on the epistyle, but even here we cannot distinguish them one from another except as "old man," "young woman," "mother" or "warrior." As for the locality in which the scenes figured here take place, and which remains totally indeterminate, we shall have occasion to speak of this in a later chapter.

The remarkable thing is that this indeterminateness, this resolute avoidance of anything that might appear as too individual, does not in any way detract from the impression of life and reality. With regard to portraiture, but the same may be said of Greek art as a whole, the words of Paul Valéry have often been quoted: "Tel qu'en lui-même l'éternité le change." But eternity in this case is not the eternity of death: it appears on the contrary to render more intense and significant the very life of those whom Greek sculptors strove, so successfully, to immortalize.

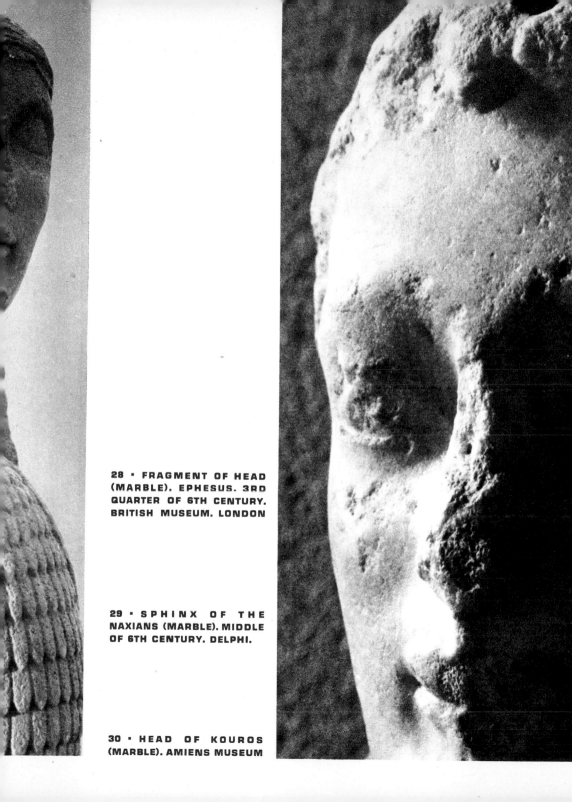

28 · FRAGMENT OF HEAD
(MARBLE). EPHESUS. 3RD
QUARTER OF 6TH CENTURY.
BRITISH MUSEUM. LONDON

29 · SPHINX OF THE
NAXIANS (MARBLE). MIDDLE
OF 6TH CENTURY. DELPHI.

30 · HEAD OF KOUROS
(MARBLE). AMIENS MUSEUM

Other features too might be mentioned as being common to Greek plastic art from the beginning to the end of its existence. But rather than enumerate them here, we shall confine ourselves to indicating those which, in different periods, or rather in different centers of production, were peculiar to the various branches of the Greek people. We have already had occasion to contrast the Doric and the Ionic. This comparison is generally applied only to architectural forms, but the contrast is also indicative of a mental outlook which finds clear expression in sculpture also.

It is a well-known fact that the Doric spirit prevailed above all on the mainland of Greece, and particularly in the Peloponnesian peninsula which marks its southern extremity, in southern Italy and Sicily, and in certain islands such as Crete. The typical Dorian spirit finds its clearest expression in the character and way of life of the Spartans, in their love of athletics, their passion for physical effort, their self-discipline often carried to the point of ruthlessness, their sense of form and their laconic manner of expression.

The Ionian spirit prevailed over the whole coast of Asia Minor, and in most of the islands that dot the Aegean Sea; here we find, if not exactly indolence and effeminacy, at least a certain agreeable complaisance, and a love of worldly pleasures. Although athleticism is as popular here as all over the Hellenic world, at least the aim is suppleness rather than strength. Logic is not neglected, but not too fine a point is put on it, and the fascinating tales of Herodotus show us what pleasure the Ionians took in digression, not to mention gossip.

It is generally recognised that it was precisely the blending of these two ways of looking at life, which are not in fact separated by any sharply-defined frontier, that produced the Attic spirit, embodying as it does both ease and simplicity and even a taste for decorative effect, a serious outlook on life and at the same time a quick response to humor.

Even within the Dorian and Ionian spheres of influence, many distinctions may be made, and various schools, or at least art centers have been recognised. The task is not an easy one for any period, especially for Hellenistic times, when we come up against almost insuperable difficulties. It is however not too fanciful to recognise in the archaic period, that is, at a time when artists were striving particularly to overcome purely technical difficulties, processes and styles characteristic of various schools, and even a certain diversity of outlook that enables us to distinguish one art center from another.

In the Dorian world many differences may be noted between the so-called colonial productions of Sicily and Greater Greece, and those of the Peloponnese. Some scholars have perhaps gone a little too far in their efforts to discriminate, but works of well attested origin show us that differences did indeed exist between the productions of, say, Argos and Sicyon, or Sicyon and Sparta. Similarly, while the large output of the school of Chios was truly Ionian in character, it appears to us far more refined and sensitive than the products of the no less Ionian school of Miletus.

We shall not go into greater detail with regard to these differences, but the point to be stressed is that Greek art appears to us so live and so varied precisely because in all parts of the Hellenic

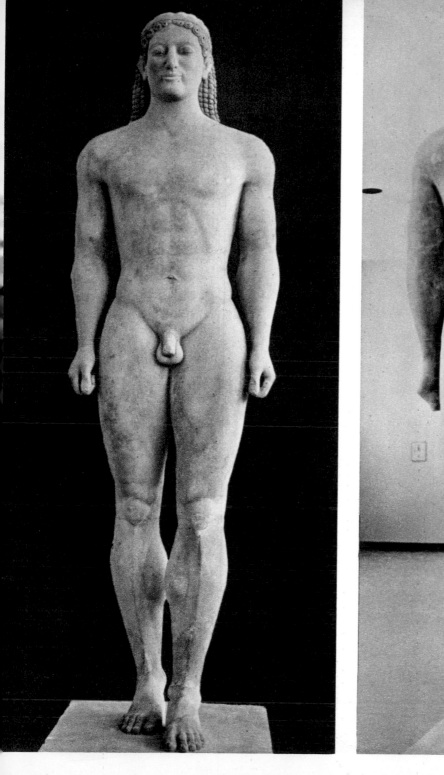
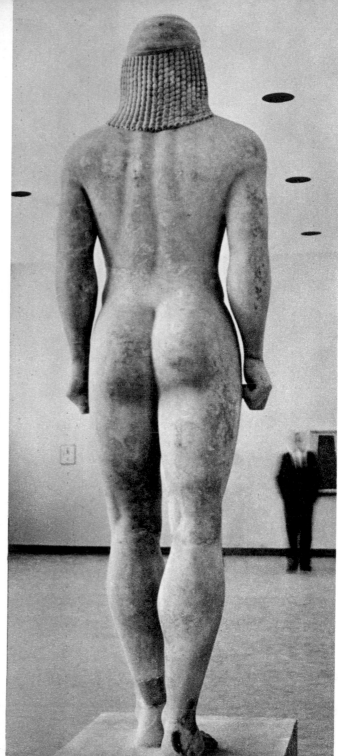

world, and sometimes in the most insignificant city-states, there were artists who sought to express, in their own way, an ideal that was common to Hellenism as a whole.

Let us now consider how this ideal which, as we have shown, was compounded of reason and moderation, and which remained closely related to man himself, the measure of all things, was expressed in various ways from the beginning to the end of Greek art.

There are several ways of looking at works of art, either the works themselves or photographic reproductions of them. We may, on the one hand, contemplate each work separately for its own sake, out of its context, considering its own intrinsic value with no thought for the period that produced it. But we may also, on the other hand, try to find in a statue or relief, the stamp of its period, in short, to set the artist's creation in its historical context, and this is what we propose to do here.

ARCHAIC SCULPTURE

Almost a century ago, people were wont to speak admiringly of what was called the "Greek miracle." But the hundreds of archaic works which systematic excavation has brought to light over the last few generations were not then known, and it was popularly supposed that Greek art did not come into being before the sixth century, the conclusion being that an art which, to judge by the few examples then known, was considered barbarous, had become so transformed in the space of a few score years as to result in the masterpieces of the Parthenon.

This theory is no longer tenable. Greek art constantly followed the line of development which is normally that of all human art. It began in fact in a childish form, and centuries were to pass before sculptors or painters achieved the mastery that we admire in the classical period.

Greek sculpture did not rise suddenly out of nothing. It was constantly inspired by foreign models, and it may be generally noted that the creative spirit among the Greeks needed contact with foreign inspiration in order to produce its masterpieces. Among its models, we may pass over the few works of sculpture produced by the Creto-Mycenaean civilization, for we have already shown how, in comparison with painting, which was intensively cultivated, plastic art had played a merely secondary role. Neither the bowed figurines of worshippers, nor the figures of young women in bell-shaped dresses with low-cut bodices, seem to have been known to the people who gradually conquered and settled down in Greece about the tenth century B.C. The movement that is apparent in the famous ivory figurine of an acrobat, among others, has no counterpart in the works of Homer's time nor in the centuries immediately following.

It was quite a different spirit which inspired the earliest truly Hellenic statuettes that have come to light. Of these, we may cite in particular a few female figures, entirely nude, and wearing a high ritual headdress called the polos: they are carved in ivory, and were discovered in a tomb

36 · TRITOPATOR. DETAIL OF A FIGURE ON THE PEDIMENT OF THE ANCIENT TEMPLE OF ATHENA (TUFA). 2ND QUARTER OF 6TH CENTURY ACROPOLIS MUSEUM. ATHENS

37 · DISCUS BEARER : FRAGMENT OF FUNERARY STELE (MARBLE).
ATTICA. 3RD QUARTER OF 6TH CENTURY. NATIONAL MUSEUM. ATHENS

38 · FACE OF KOUROS (LIMESTONE). SANCTUARY OF APOLLO PTOIOS.
BOEOTIA. MIDDLE OF 6TH CENTURY. NATIONAL MUSEUM. ATHENS

39 · HEAD OF KORE (MARBLE). ABOUT 530. ACROPOLIS MUSEUM. ATHENS

40 · HEAD OF RIDER KNOWN AS " RAMPIN HEAD " (MARBLE).
ATHENS. MIDDLE OF 6TH CENTURY. LOUVRE MUSEUM. PARIS

41 · HEAD OF KORE (MARBLE). ABOUT 520. ACROPOLIS MUSEUM. ATHENS

at Athens. It is generally agreed that they date back as far as the ninth century B.C., and it has been supposed that the several figurines all represent a goddess whose protection was sought by the deceased. The material used, at a time when trade with Syria was not yet established on a regular basis, the nudity which is unusual in Greek representations of the female figure, and the polos which is an Eastern form of headdress, have led scholars to wonder whether these idols were really produced in Greece, and not rather brought over by some traveller from abroad. In point of fact these tiny pieces could so easily have been slipped into a sailor's bundle, but whatever their origin, these statues unquestionably bear the stamp of the East which, at the beginning of the first millenium B.C., might justifiably have appeared as the very model of civilization to the simple Balkan peoples who had migrated slowly towards the southern limits of the Peloponnese. In any case, there is a marked contrast between these figures and other purely local figures of horses and oxen which strike us as particularly stiff and uninspired.

The influence of the East is even more apparent in larger scale modelling. This form of art came into being, as we have already seen, only when Eastern and Egyptian models inspired Greek sculptors with the idea of carving stone images of much greater size than the figurines. And the very manner in which the sculptors went about their task shows us that they were taking their lead from abroad.

Two types in fact, and two only, were favoured by sculptors and their clients for almost a century. On the one hand, the figure of a man in a standing position, nude, and seen from the front — a figure which might equally well be a god, a deceased person or a worshipper dedicating his own image to the Immortals. The nudity is explained by the fact that Greek athletes were naked while taking part in contests, and that, from Homer's time onwards, it was generally thought that the highest form of beauty was that of the male body trained by gymnastics and intelligently developed. This represents the truly Hellenic feature in this type of statuary. As far as the rest is concerned, it is rather Egyptian statues that come to mind when we look at these tall young men standing firmly on both feet, the left leg slightly in advance of the right, their arms stiffly at their sides, their head erect, and their thick locks of hair falling on their shoulders. Even the rather solid proportions of some of the figures recall those of the statues which the Egyptians dedicated in their temples, and the Egyptian influence is very apparent in one characteristic detail: to the Greeks the left side was the unlucky side, and if these statues all have the left foot rather than the right in front, it is because figures were made that way in the Nile Valley.

This virile type, a man without individual features who, for this reason, is nowadays designated simply as "youth" (kouros), served as a starting-point for the Greeks' study of anatomy. Even in their first attempts, the proportions are on the whole fairly correct, and this is no doubt partly due to the fact that, by studying easily transportable models of smaller dimensions, the sculptors had only to repeat the general position of the Egyptian statues. But precisely because they drew their inspiration, not from originals which they had no means of going to see on the spot, but from small-scale models of great Egyptian works, they were left to their own resources in the matter of details. Thus we find them groping their way over a long period. They realized quite well where the difficulties lay, but they did not know how to overcome them. They knew that the human torso is made up of a certain number of segments divided down the middle by a vertical line passing through the navel, and cut horizontally by the folds of the aponeuroses. But such knowledge has something of the abstract and intellectual about it: they neither saw nor felt the complex inter-play of the muscles: they established it by an effort of the intellect, which consequently resulted in a diagrammatical representation very different from actual fact. Sometimes the thorax is repre-sented as a kind of pointed arch, and the ribs resemble the bones of a fish; sometimes the number of segments is greater than in reality. In particular, Greek sculptors took a long time to grasp the idea of volume, and it was by incising lines on the stone that they indicated details on an essen-tially plane surface. Certain parts were especially difficult, such as the knee and the ear, and by

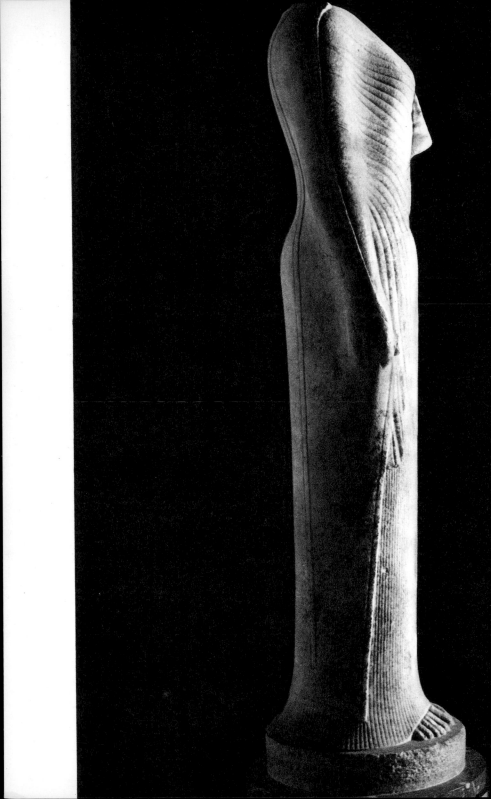

43 · STATUE DEDICATED TO HERA BY CHERAMYES (MARBLE). SAMOS. MIDDLE OF 6TH CENTURY. LOUVRE MUSEUM. PARIS

44 · 45 · KOUROS OF THE SANCTUARY OF APOLLO PTOIOS (MARBLE). BOEOTIA. MIDDLE OF 6TH CENTURY. NATIONAL MUSEUM. ATHENS

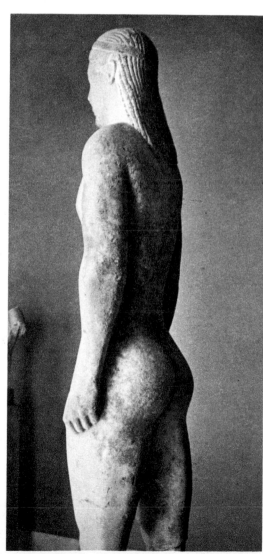

46 · COMBAT OF THE GODS AND GIANTS

47 · DETAIL OF ATHENA

noting the manner in which they sought to solve these problems, we may try to recognise the hand, the procedure, one might even say the tricks, of a particular artist or school.

To this masculine type of the kouros corresponds a female type just as stereotyped, and also inspired by the East, the kore or young woman. She is never represented nude, for women in Greece, except to a certain extent in Sparta, took no part in athletic contests nor physical exercises. She is, on the contrary, dressed in her finest clothes, and according to the region and also to the fashion of the times, she may be severely draped in the Dorian peplum, or else swathed in the finer, softer material of the himation. The posture is the same as that of the kouros. Nor should this surprise us, in view of the fact that, whether the kore is an idol or the image of a worshipper, the figure is always seen in a ceremonial atmosphere, in an almost ritually hieratic attitude, facing the spectator.

This front view is one of the rules of primitive art and all these figures, when due account is taken of the forward position of one leg and occasionally a bend in one arm, are strictly symmetrical in conception, in relation to an imaginary axis. This certainly results in a rigidity which appears to detract from the impression of life, but should we be justified in attributing this to the inexperience of the artist? Is it not rather a desired effect, which helps to give the figures a solemnity appropriate to religious offerings? Nor is this rigidity confined to the bodily posture only: for a very long time the face remained entirely devoid of expression, the eyes being usually very large and, as is characteristic of Greek sculpture in the archaic period, exaggeratedly round and protruding. The exophthalmus of these figures has often been commented upon. Should this also be attributed to lack of skill? The technical problems confronting the sculptors cannot be overlooked, but these staring eyes and the rigidity of the facial expression are neverthless appropriate to the human being face to face with his god. In a general way, the resolutely ceremonial character of these figures must be stressed, and even the coquetry they suggest indicates that they were careful with their appearance in order to please the Immortal, or to win the admiration of human spectators. This coquetry is not restricted to the women, with their embroidered dresses and their ear-rings. The elaborate hair style is common to both sexes, and lent itself to the same tricks of arrangement for the reason that, at this period, both men and women wore their hair long.

48 · TREASURE HOUSE OF SIPHNOS, DETAIL OF NORTH FRIEZE. APOLLO AND ARTEMIS STRUGGLING WITH THREE GIA

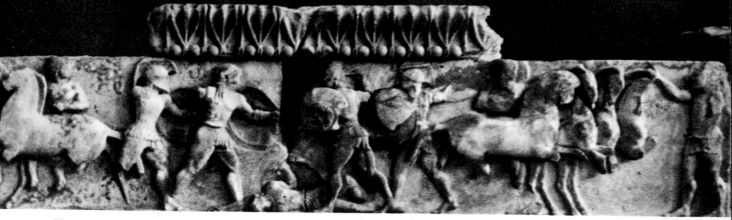

49 · TREASURE HOUSE OF SIPHNOS. EAST FRIEZE (MARBLE). ABOUT 525. DELPHI

50 · DETAIL OF EAST FRIEZE. APHRODITE. ARTEMIS. APOLLO

Let us glance at some of the works produced in Attica at the time of Pisistratus. The desire to present a pleasing appearance became, at that period, more pronounced. The facial expression is animated, and lit up by a wide smile which, however, is in some cases rather vacuous. Previous generations of scholars have discussed this smile at some length, and have seen in it the expression of a whole philosophical outlook. The explanation is a simpler one. The impassivity of ancient statues seemed over-simplified to the more acute and sophisticated minds of this period; they wanted to show that a human being has a soul and a capacity for feeling.

Technically speaking, the two simplest ways of conveying feeling in a carved figure as in a painted one, are to draw the lips upwards or downwards. Drawing them downwards gives a pouting expression which would ill become either a benevolent deity or a human being anxious to please. Drawing them upwards results in a smile, and this was the manner chosen. It became a mere formula, so familiar to artists that, much later on, on the pediments at Aegina, they could even give a smile to the dying.

The introduction of the smile and the idea of giving an intelligent expression to the face are not the only innovations that may be ascribed to the latter half of the sixth century. It was during this period that the Greeks developed that sense of full relief without which there is no sculpture worthy of the name, and which enables the artist, through the play of light and shade, to bring out the irregularities and movements of the human body. Another innovation, and a no less important one, was, in fact, the introduction of movement. It must, however, be borne in mind that, from the very beginnings of sculpture, movement had not been totally unknown. As the artist began to feel a growing mastery over the stone he was working, he would, somewhat hesitantly, separate one of the arms from the trunk, or detach one of the hands which had hitherto always lain along the thigh or across the breast; he would even, in some cases, pivot the torso slightly from the waist. But it was not really until about 550 that greater freedom was introduced into bodily attitudes. New types of statues make their appearance, breaking away from the traditional front view. The Moschophorus, or man carrying a calf for sacrifice, is still quite rigid. But less than a generation later, on the Acropolis at Athens, a young nobleman dedicated his image after winning a horse race. He is to be seen mounted on his horse, and as he parades up and down after his victory, he is turning his head to one side towards the spectators who are applauding him. Of course, the particular theme chosen by the artist calls for this movement, but he had to be capable of rendering it.

It was not from lack of skill, or because movement "breaks the line," that so many years passed before figures sculptured in the round showed some signs of life. For proof, we have only to look at the great number of reliefs sculptured throughout the sixth century, for in reliefs, as in vase-painting, artists had from early days delighted in depicting in a lively manner momentary attitudes.

One of the most ancient reliefs known to us once decorated the pediment of the temple of Artemis on Corfu. Its composition appears strange: in the center of it, directly under the point

of the roof, is the vast and monstrous figure of the Gorgon. With her hair bristling with serpents, tongue hanging out and jaws wide open in a distorted and inhuman face, she is there to frighten away evil spirits — a figure that is of magical rather than religious significance. On either side of her are two fierce lionesses, then Pegasus, then Zeus striking down a Giant, and a goddess, Ge the Earth Mother no doubt, threatened by an enemy; right in the angle is a fine recumbent figure. There is no unity in the whole, neither of subject nor, it might be said, of style. There is a marked contrast between the immobility of the Gorgon and the two beasts on either side of her, and the lively movement of Zeus striking down his adversary with a rapid and well-aimed blow. Other movements, of a different nature, were depicted at approximately the same time, about 575, on small pediments of the Acropolis at Athens, where we see Hercules at close grips with one of his enemies, or a lion striking down and devouring a bull. In these cases, it is not merely a matter of gesture; the very rendering of the muscles indicates an inward striving and force which are never to be found in the statues of the kouroi and kores.

The same striving after power and movement, that is manifest in the very disposition of the body and the muscles even more than in the posture itself, is to be seen in the few isolated metopes that have come down to us from the Treasure-house dedicated by the city of Sicyon to Apollo at Delphi. It is difficult to decide which is the more typical, that which depicts solely a boar run to earth and about to rush at his pursuers, or that which is apparently less dramatic, on which Castor, Pollux and one of their companions coming back from a raid, are pacing along with the

cattle they have carried off. These metopes form one of the most typical examples of Doric art in the sixth century: with their controlled passion and relentless will to overcome, these figures, animated by an inner driving force, have no need of dramatic gesture to impress on us their irresistible movement.

It is not because they are some twenty-five years later in date that the reliefs sculptured about 425 on the frieze of the Treasure-house dedicated, also at Delphi, by the small but wealthy city of Siphnos, leave us with quite a different impression, for these are characteristic of the Ionian spirit. Four themes are represented one after another on a continous border running round the tiny building. Two of them are particularly successful, the one representing the battle of the Gods and Giants, and the other the battle of the Greeks and Trojans. The movements in these cases are, if not exactly disorderly, at least expressively violent. The artist's aim has been to interest us directly in his characters, and to this end he has varied as far as possible their costume, their posture and even, although they are fairly small-sized figures, their expression. In the middle of the scene depicting the struggle between the Greeks and the Trojans, the Gods are represented as deciding the outcome of the battle, discussing heatedly the great exploits being

54 · TREASURE HOUSE OF SIPHNOS. SOUTH FRIEZE. CARRYING OFF OF THE DAUGHTERS OF LEUCIPPES : DETAIL.
55 · DETAIL OF THE CHARIOT HORSES

performed on the earth beneath them by heroes who have been carefully differentiated by the inscription of their names. It is a triumph of the picturesque, but without sentimentality, and resulting from an intelligent, and in some respects humorous, observation of gesture and attitude.

The effect of the whole scene was heightened by the use of color, which was still bright at the time when these reliefs were unearthed. Nor is this surprising, since all ancient Greek sculpture was painted in vivid colors, in brilliant red and blue: patches of black and gold highlighted this color scheme which was not intended to be realistic but merely to accentuate forms by the contrasts it set up. It must also be mentioned that certain elements in a different material, bronze for example, were often added to a work of sculpture — the spears brandished by the warriors and the chariot wheels were not sculptured in stone but fashioned separately in metal and added afterwards.

An academic love of Greece should not blind us to the naively barbaric element in compositions of this nature. Seventeenth century good taste would no doubt have been shocked by the spontaneous impetuosity of this art of the time of Pisistratus which we, on the contrary, admire almost unreservedly. For we find in these works an unsophisticated freshness showing the artists' passionate desire to depict life as they saw it with their own eyes, and to portray feelings which

TREASURE HOUSE OF SIPHNOS. EAST PEDIMENT (MARBLE). ABOUT 525. DELPHI

56 · APOLLO AND HERACLES CONTESTING THE TRIPOD

57 · A SOLDIER

were perhaps not very profound, but at least were genuinely human. It is with a total lack of self-consciousness that the kore who is dedicating herself to Athena on the Acropolis seeks to please the goddess with her smile, her somewhat countrified charm and the trouble she has taken over her dress. It is with justifiable pride that the nude kouros displays to the god a body perfected by intelligent exercise. There is a wholeheartedness in the manner in which warriors and hunters strive with all their might to get the better of their adversaries. It must be admitted that some of the figures of this period are not entirely free from affectation, but this very affectation has a certain child-like quality about it which is not displeasing. It is impossible to remain unmoved in the face of this exuberant vitality.

This art has all the more appeal for us in that it lasted so short a time. The sixth century was not yet at its close before new trends appeared in the art as well as in the outlook of the Greeks. Already dark clouds were gathering on the horizon. In the city-states, responsibilities which had hitherto been borne by the leading citizens or by those dictators known as tyrants, were now assumed by the citizens as a body. From outside, a great Asian power, the Persian empire, was casting covetous glances towards the Hellenic world. Lightheartedness was a thing of the past: serious reflection was taking its place.

It was about this time that fashions themselves began to change. Men no more wore their hair long and caught up in a chignon on the nape of the neck. It was then too that sculptors, less optimistic now in their outlook on life, gradually abandoned the set smile in order to give the face a more thoughtful expression, which sometimes even gave an impression of disdain or sulkiness.

At the same time, religious feeling became more intense; people became more than ever aware of the respect owing to the gods. We no longer find temples being decorated in such a way that the sole purpose would seem to be to delight the visitor with beautiful pictures. When a large marble pediment was added to the dwelling-place of Apollo at Delphi through the generous gift of a great Athenian family, the Alcmaeonidae, it showed the god himself, with his sister Artemis and his mother Leto, appearing in all his glory for the edification of the faithful. Similarly, on the Acropolis at Athens, the theme chosen for the façade of the temple of Athena was the triumph of the Olympians over the rebellious Giants.

Religious too, though in a slightly different sense, were the steles placed on the tombs of the dead, and which at this period were tall and narrow, bearing only the single image of the person buried there. The intention was not, as in our own time, to offer visitors to the cemetery an exact portrait, with all his decorations, of a man who did not want to be forgotten. Far from it: the individual desired, even after his death, to be considered as merely a part of the social group to which he belonged, and all these steles depict a strictly limited number of types. According to the deceased's social status, his image graven in low relief on the stele would be that of a warrior, or an old man offering a grasshopper to his dog — in this case he was no doubt a landed proprietor — or else a young man of some refinement holding in his fingers, as in so many vase-paintings of the period, a graceful flower. It is neverthless a religious monument, it must be repeated, for the dead were, if not actually gods, at least superior to mortal men, and would seek vengeance if they

58 · KORE (POLYCHROME MAR-
BLE). CHIOS. ABOUT 510. ACRO-
POLIS MUSEUM. ATHENS

were not paid due honor by those who survived them.

Are we to assume that this religious significance was responsible for the serious expression we find on the persons figuring on the steles? It would of course be quite out of place to represent the dead on their tombstones as radiant with joy, but in actual fact these persons who have just died are treated in exactly the same spirit as those whose statues were sculptured in the round, at the same period, as votive offerings.

We must, however, make a distinction between lofty art and minor art. Not all works are stamped with religious feeling, and when they have no ritual significance, the artists gave much freer rein to their

59 · EPHEBES AT LEISURE. DOG AND CAT FIGHTING

SCENES FROM THE PALAESTRA. (MARBLE). LATE 6TH CENTURY. NATIONAL MUSEUM. ATHENS

60 · HIGH JUMP. WRESTLING. JAVELIN THROWING

fancy. We have only to glance at the painted vases of the period, the decoration being composed of picturesque scenes, very realistic and frequently even licentious; why indeed should artists have been too serious when it was not the gods who were intended to look on their work? At any rate, though the sculptor might fashion his kouros with all the seriousness demanded by current religious sentiment, he felt himself much freer when decorating with reliefs the base supporting the statue. The National Museum in Athens possesses one of these pedestals, decorated on its three visible sides with scenes taken from the life of young men: on the right and on the left, they are practising high jump, wrestling or discus-throwing; in the center they are at rest, interestedly watching a dog fighting a cat — little pictures of daily life whose simplicity and familiarity must have contrasted sharply with the austere grandeur of the statue, unfortunately lost to us, which towered above them.

The gravity we find in both the posture and the facial expression of the monumental figures of this period still remains a little vague and ill-defined; it creates an atmosphere, but does not yet correspond to any visible emotion. Although the face is no longer smiling, it cannot be said, for all that, to be sad, and the eyes are still rather too vague to give an impression of inward reflection. Yet one may catch a hint of what the artist was trying to convey, that is, depth of feeling; artists were moving away from the simplicity that we find in the friezes of the Treasure-house of Siphnos, and were trying to tackle the great problems that confront humanity, while at the same time philosophers and learned men were working out their theories of the nature of the world and of mankind. There was a growing awareness that previous generations had taken an over-simplified view of the world. But to convey these more complex feelings, artists came up against technical difficulties as yet unresolved. By the end of the century substantial progress had undoubt-edly been made, but more particularly in the matter of the treatment of anatomy and drapery. Through constant repetition, over half a century, of the same models and the same attitudes, artists had gradually succeeded in making their work more realistic, and in mastering, one after the other, the problems that had disconcerted them in the beginning. It is, in fact, curious to note that sculp-tors acquired this mastery in small stages. With an almost child-like concentration, they had attacked each detail separately, and they were still reproducing the structure of a torso with a great many errors when they had already learned to fashion surely and gracefully the fine joints of a toe or finger.

Drapery too had presented perhaps even more serious problems than the actual structure of the body. If the Dorian peplum, with its rather heavy material falling in regular vertical folds held by their own weight, followed more or less the general lines of the body, the woollen tunic (chiton) on the other hand, and the great cloak or himation which served as an over-garment, were far more complicated and difficult both in themselves and in their relation to each other. Attempts have often been made in our own time to drape a living model exactly as certain kores from the Acropolis were draped. Such attempts are foredoomed to failure, for in actual fact sculptors did not aim at a photographic exactness of detail. No doubt in their heart of hearts they would have liked to achieve it, but realising that they were incapable of doing so, they contented them-selves with giving an outward impression of truth. It must be admitted that they very often succeed-ed, and if the historian of costume is thereby sometimes disappointed, at least those who look at these works from a mere love of beauty are completely taken in by the illusion of truth. What would perhaps shock such persons is the fact that the stuff which they know and feel to be soft and light is in many cases very stiff and has the rigid appearance of a metallic drapery.

61 · KORE (MARBLE). ABOUT 500. ACROPOLIS MUSEUM. ATHENS

Many of the observations we have made above may be applied most particularly to the art of Athens. And even if Athens is not yet, in spite of its glory in the reign of Pisistratus, the spiritual capital of Greece, it is in fact one of the cities in which art found its most dazzling expression. But we have seen, when we were speaking of the metopes of the Treasure-house of Sicyon or the frieze of the Treasure-house of Siphnos, that there were schools purely Ionian, or purely Dorian, which were also outstanding.

Mention must also be made of the production of more distant art centers. Certain reliefs discovered at Selinus in Sicily have the same vigorous quality, in a rather more rustic context, as the sculpture of the Peloponnese. From this region we possess various monuments which are in many respects more characteristic than those of Greece proper, and whose aesthetic value is almost equal.

But is there anything to be gained by emphasizing the differences between the various schools of the archaic period? It is surely more profitable, for those of us who are not archaeologists, to examine the features that are common to all schools from the beginning to the end of the Greek archaic period. In all of them we find the same passionate striving to get closer to reality, the same desire to impart life to their works. That this conception of life was not identical on the fringes of Asia Minor, in the heart of the Peloponnese,

in far-off Sicily and on the Acropolis at Athens, is of little moment. It was after all only to be expected that the sculptors of the Cyclades should have represented the outward appearance of athletes less faithfully and less vigorously than the mainland Greeks whose champions year after year carried off the palm of victory. It is natural too that the smile should first have appeared on statues from Ionia and at the court of Pisistratus where so many Ionians were favourably received. Not all the Greeks had the same things to say, but all of them showed the same desire to clothe their thoughts in concrete reality, and to avoid all that was mysterious, ill-defined or illogical. When technical difficulties prevented them from giving a strictly realistic form to their ideas, they were not above a slight deception, but always keeping as close as possible to the exact form of what they were trying to express. Dorians, Ionians or Athenians, those of the great centers or of the remote provinces, all alike with constant alertness of mind, with an ingenuity worthy of a Daedalus or a Ulysses, strove to make their creations the closest possible representations of reality.

62 · ATTIC-IONIAN KORE (MARBLE). ACROPOLIS MUSEUM, ATHENS

63 · HEAD OF KORE (MARBLE). MIDDLE OF 6TH CENTURY. ACROPOLIS MUSEUM. ATHENS

64 · WOMAN WITH POMEGRANATE (MARBLE). 2ND HALF OF 6TH CENTURY. ACROPOLIS MUSEUM. ATHENS

THE PRE-CLASSICAL PERIOD

The years 480-478 B.C., when the Persian armies that had invaded Greece were being pushed back towards Asia, may be considered as marking a turning-point in Hellenic history. Once freed from the peril that had threatened them, the Greeks emerged from the experience with a new-found maturity, and the archaic period is generally considered to have come to an end at this time.

In actual fact, this delineation is no more sharply defined than any other. In the years immediately preceding the final victory, works of art were being created which in many respects were tied to past traditions, and which yet cannot confidently be reckoned as wholly archaic. Again at Delphi, yet another Treasure-house which, like those of the Siphnians and the Sicyonians, was used for storing the offerings of the citizens whose state had dedicated it, was erected by the Athenians shortly after the battle of Marathon in 490. The frieze of this small building of the Doric order was decorated with scenes in relief which, in certain details, are so traditional in manner as to appear to belong to about 510 B.C. in spite of the inscription mentioning the battle of Marathon. Yet, in other respects, the scenes dealing with the legends of Theseus and Heracles are so much in advance of their times as to foreshadow the type of art that was to develop after 480. It has been observed that the reliefs were executed by an artist who had placed himself at the spectators' standpoint, and has calculated the effect his work would produce when viewed

65 · 66 · THESEUS CARRYING OFF ANTIOPE (MARBLE). GROUP FROM PEDIMENT OF THE TEMPLE OF APOLLO AT ERETRIA (EUBOEA). ABOUT 510. CHALCIS MUSEUM

from below and under certain well-determined light conditions — an artistic refinement of which no previous example is known. Furthermore, certain metopes, such as that which depicts Theseus confronting Athena, are, by reason of their composition, distribution of masses and simplicity of line, of a purity that even the classical period at its best could not surpass. Admittedly, alongside these, other reliefs are still laboring under the traditions of the past. And in particular, what gives these works their archaic character is that detail is very rarely subordinated to the general plan. The artist has in almost all cases juxtaposed sections, each of which has been worked with the same elaborate care. He has not yet acquired that sense of overall effect which demands the sacrifice of less important details in order to bring out the features that must first strike attention.

Another work of the transitional period, in that it too embodies both archaic and modernizing tendencies, is the decoration of the temple which the Aeginetans dedicated on their island to their tutelary goddess Aphaia, probably in the years immediately preceding 480. The two pediments are composed in identical fashion: in the center stands the goddess Aphaia presiding over a combat taking place in the two angles. This is no battle mêlée, but isolated groups placed alongside one another, a series of duels, so that the unity of the whole lies solely in the fact that all the figures represented are warriors fighting. The artists have made clever use of the framework imposed on them, and figures bending forward in a defensive attitude, a kneeling archer stringing his bow, or the dead lying prostrate on the ground, follow out the lines of the roof-slope right to the corners. Between the two pediments, there may be noted certain differences of style

67 · DANCING GIRLS (SANDSTONE). METOPE FROM THE TEMPLE OF HERA, AT THE MOUTH OF THE RIVER SELE. LAST QUARTER OF 6TH CENTURY. PAESTUM MUSEUM. ITALY

68 · THE WARRIOR ARISTION. FUNERARY STELE (MARBLE). ATTICA. LATE 6TH CENTURY. NATIONAL MUSEUM. ATHENS

which are not readily accounted for, and it might easily be imagined that some twenty years had elapsed between the execution of the two. The most probable explanation is that the Aeginetans engaged two sculptors, one of whom remained faithful to traditions already out of date, while the other belonged to a more advanced school of thought. This is one of the most interesting features of the monument in question, for we can see here the meeting of two trends which no doubt co-existed for a considerable time before the newer one prevailed. The parts that have come to light, and are at present housed in the Munich Museum, were too much restored at the time of their discovery for us to be able to venture a judgment on the style of the two sculptors. But the stiff hieratical attitude of the goddess on the west front contrasts with the already classical freedom of the attitudes of the combatants. We are still a long way from the Discobolus, but we can at least get some indication of the lines along which sculpture was developing.

The Persians had hardly been driven out of Greece when Athens, the city that was hardest hit by the war, was swept by a wave of intense patriotism. Though smoke was still rising from the ruins, two sculptors, whose names we possess, Critios and Nesiotes, had already been engaged to sculpture the figures of Harmodius and Aristogiton, the two men who had tried to rid their state of the illegal regime of tyrants, and to win Athens her freedom. We need not here lay stress on the political character of this enterprise, at a moment when Athens had delivered Greece from a foreign yoke. What is more important, is that this group, which we know from copies and from vase-paintings of it, affords the first example of two figures united by a common action. They are side by side, but facing different ways, one of them three-quarters turned to the right and the other to the left, their movements are interrelated as if they were obeying a command given by one of them, and in the expression of both (one is a man of mature age and the other still a youth) may be read the same resolute determination. The group was set up in one of the busiest parts of Athens, which explains the immobility of the figures who seem to have arrested their movement suddenly to attract the attention of the crowd. Their legs are apart as if they are walking, but they have both feet firmly planted on the ground; they are brandishing weapons, but their outstretched arms are motionless, and they seem to be proferring their chests to be struck by the city guards who will punish their crime.

The same immobility is, for many years, to be met with only in figures which are also set up for public admiration. In saying this, we are thinking particularly of one of the few large-sized bronzes we possess from the fifth century, the Charioteer, discovered at Delphi. This statue belonged to a group, the rest of which has been lost. He was mounted on his chariot, and was holding the reins of the four horses harnessed to it. Beside him must have stood the owner of the team, tyrant of a town in Sicily, who was considered as the true winner of the race. No doubt the charioteer, clothed in the very long robe which was the uniform of his profession, was turning towards the crowd who were acclaiming the tyrant, but his bearing is modest and

69 HERACLES (MARBLE). FIGURE FROM THE EAST PEDIMENT OF THE TEMPLE OF APHAIA AT AEGINA. 1ST QUARTER OF 5TH CENTURY. GLYPTOTHEK OF MUNICH

the battle was a mere series of single combats, the groups being clearly separated one from another, each treated as a single unit, as if the various parts were completed in a workroom and then set up together on the top of the temple. At Olympia, there is a continuous movement which, without the slightest interruption, seems to carry on from the center to the corners of the tympanum. Even when they do not actually touch, the figures carry over from the group to which they belong into the next one; the movements are combined in such a way as to merge into a general pattern which the eye unconsciously follows from end to end, and the action of each figure blends into the general movement of the whole. Whereas, in the preparation for the chariot race, the facial expression of the actors remained almost inscrutable, here the feelings are very clearly shown, at least in the case of the Lapithae who, as a barbarian people, knew no reserve or self-control, which are qualities of civilized races. Bitten by the young woman whom he is trying to carry off, one of the Centaurs is howling with pain, and the human masks of these half-beasts may be compared with those theater masks, expressive of violent emotion, which at the same period were worn by actors so that the audience might be clearly aware of the emotions the playwright wished to portray.

All the figures of the pediments are, as indeed at Aegina too, sculptured in the round, standing well away from the wall which formed the background of the tympanum, and the marble was painted in as violent colors as in the archaic period, so that in the sunlight details could be more easily distinguished. Although well removed from the eye-level of the spectators, and intended to be viewed from afar, the figures are treated with as much care as if they had been displayed on ground level. And the artists' consummate skill can be seen as much in the scope of the overall composition as in the delicate rendering of the muscles, the lines of wrinkles and the admirable delineation of the hands. The drapery is rather on the heavy side, but is perfectly adapted to the lines of the body which it fills out most convincingly.

A similar skill may be recognised in the metopes which are in relief, though fairly high relief. Each of the twelve bronze plaques deals with one of the labors of Heracles, a hero dear to the whole of Greece, but whom the Dorians considered as being more particularly their own. Even more perhaps than the pediments, these metopes reveal the changes that were taking place in Greek thought. In some cases Heracles is shown accomplishing one of his feats, aided by the active though invisible presence of his protectress, Athena. But in other cases we can see him, when his task is over, joyfully carrying on his wrist the birds he had captured at the Stymphalian lake, or else — and unfortunately this is one of the most badly damaged metopes — gazing reflectively, as if overwhelmed, at the lifeless body of the Nemean lion, dismayed, one might say, by the prospect of all the labors still awaiting him. The time is long past when he was represented as a hero of brute strength, triumphing effortlessly, and, once the feat was accomplished, thinking only of his food and pleasure. Heracles has become the symbol of mankind continually struggling, and achieving happiness only after triumphing over increasingly difficult obstacles.

The high moral ideal expressed in the temple at Olympia is that of the whole period around the year 450. It was about this time that a relief was made to be dedicated to the divinities of Eleusis, representing Demeter, the great dispenser of fertility, handing over to the young Athenian Triptolemus, in the presence of her daughter Core, the ear of corn which he was to distribute among men to teach them to cultivate the earth and to grow wheat. From a technical point of view, this work is devoid of any trace of archaism, but the artist, being perhaps a trifle hesitant as yet, a little anxious about the effect he might produce, may be said to have purposely refrained from displaying to the full the virtuosity he already possessed. He left some things unsaid; the

SIDE VIEWS OF THE
" LUDOVISI THRONE "

84 · FLUTE PLAYER

85 · WOMAN BURNING
INCENSE

figures seem to suggest latent possibilities, just as, at Olympia, the figures always appeared to possess greater strength than they were actually using. The sculptor could have gone further than he did, but he chose not to do so. No doubt the artists of the time knew as well as Hesiod that often "the half is greater than the whole."

The sculptor responsible for this relief, which suggests an atmosphere of religious contemplation, is unknown to us. It has been suggested that, even if these noble figures are not from the hand of Phidias himself, they may at least be attributed to some close disciple of his. It is not impossible, for Phidias, as we know, worked at Eleusis before he became, in all matters concerning the Fine Arts, Pericles' right-hand man.

CLASSICISM

It is not relevant to our purpose to discuss here the motives which inspired the Athenians to carry out, in the city and in particular on the sacred plateau of the Acropolis, that vast series of works which employed a large part of the laboring and artisan population of Attica continuously for twenty years or so, and then somewhat less regularly up to about 410. Of the monuments erected during that brief period which has been called, since the time of Voltaire, the Age of Pericles, the only one which strictly concerns us here is the temple erected in honour of Athena, the Parthenon.

There are few buildings, at least in mainland Greece, whose sculptured ornaments reach such a high degree of perfection, and this great display of reliefs forming not a single, but a double frieze, is no doubt largely due to the temperament of Phidias. Even the very statue of Athena herself, set up for the adoration of the faithful, was covered with an enormous number of sculptured motifs.

Our understanding of these sculptures will be far from complete unless we look further than their intrinsic beauty and consider the motives that led Pericles, and consequently Phidias, to situate in a certain particular spot subjects that were not chosen at random.

86 · HERACLES CAPTURING THE BRAZEN-FOOTED HIND (MARBLE). NORTH METOPE OF THE ATHENIAN TREASURE-HOUSE AT DELPHI. 490. DELPHI

87 · DEMETER AND CORA, GLORIFICATION OF THE FLOWER (MARBLE). PHARSALUS. ABOUT 470. LOUVRE MUSEUM, PARIS

88 · DEATH OF ACTION (LIMESTONE). METOPE FROM THE TEMPLE OF HERA AT SELINUS. ABOUT 460. PALERMO MUSEUM

89 · 90 · ZEUS OR POSEI-
DON (BRONZE). ABOUT 460/
450. FOUND UNDER WATER,
OFF EUBOEA; NEAR CAPE
ARTEMISIUM. NATIONAL
MUSEUM. ATHENS

We must realize from the outset that the Parthenon, like all Greek temples, was above all the dwelling place of a deity, and that its sole purpose was to contain an idol which popular superstition considered as a living being. Now Athena, whom the political party in the ascendant about 450 wished to glorify, was not the goddess of war nor of wisdom, but the very personification and symbol of the whole Athenian people. Nothing was too extravagant for a dedication of this nature. The statue was of colossal size, since apart from the six-foot pedestal on which it rested, it stood about 40 feet high. It was not in bronze like its counterpart, the Athena Promachos, a statue no less gigantic which Phidias had made a few years before to dominate the whole city from the heights of the Acropolis; the Athena Parthenos he sculptured in gold and ivory. The gold leaf was used for the drapery, while the whiteness of ivory was used for the exposed parts of the body, the face and arms. We shall not go into a detailed description of this statue whose precious materials were re-utilised even before the end of the ancient world, and which we know only from copies of very unequal merit; even if we were to describe its appearance, we should still have no clearer idea of what constituted its universally recognized beauty. Perhaps this contrast between gold and ivory, and the numerous motifs, sphinx and winged horses, adorning her helmet, gave the idol a somewhat barbaric appearance, but by means of engraved stones and coins we are familiar with the profile of the goddess, and we can see how calm and majestically serene was her face. The shield

91 · HERMES AND THE GRACES, DANCING (MARBLE). ABOUT 500. ACROPOLIS MUSEUM, ATHENS

resting on the ground and leaning against her side was decorated on both sides; the reverse side was merely painted, but on the outer side was represented the combat between the Greeks and the Amazons. Even the sandals were decorated, the thong depicting the Lapithae fighting the Centaurs. None of these themes was arbitrarily chosen since, like the whole story of the battle of the Giants painted on the inner side of the shield, they call to mind Greek victories and the triumph of Greek civilization.

For this reason, it comes as no surprise to find that the same subjects were taken up again in greater detail on the Doric frieze which runs round the peristyle above the colonnade. The combat against the Amazons occupies the western façade; the main façade, on the eastern side, shows the battle against the Giants, and it is on the southern side, relegated to the least striking position, as to the sandals on the statue of the goddess, that we find the combat between the Lapithae and the Centaurs which did not directly concern Athenian legend. One of the main façades, the northern one, was devoted to scenes from the Trojan War, chosen, we may suppose, in order to point out the futility of war and to show the sorrow it brings in its train.

We have not as yet mentioned the fact that the great statue of Athena carried in her right hand, as if offering it to the Athenians, a statue of Victory, nor that on the pedestal, the artisans of Athens were symbolically glorified in a scene showing deities themselves, Hephaestos and

92 · HERACLES PRESENTING ATHENA WITH ONE OF THE STYMPHALIAN BIRDS. LOUVRE MUSEUM, PARIS

METOPES FROM THE TEMPLE OF ZEUS AT OLYMPIA (MARBLE) 470/456

93 · THE GOLDEN APPLES FROM THE GARDEN OF THE HESPERIDES. OLYMPIA MUSEUM

Athena, fashioning in clay with their own hands a form which, when they had bestowed life on it, was to become the first human being.

Contrary to all the rules, an Ionic frieze runs in an unbroken line round the wall enclosing the chamber containing the statue and the adjacent chamber. It depicts a real ceremony which took place at Athens every four years, and in which not only the citizens took part, but also the resident aliens, the metoikoi.

It was a real ceremony, and when we look at three sides of the building, we can well believe that, although it is presented in diagrammatic form, it none the less represents actual fact. But when we turn to the fourth side, the main façade, we find a combination of truth and fiction. For at the festival, as it actually took place, the procession of the Athenians carried up to the old temple, to place on the ancient statue of Athena, a richly embroidered mantle woven for her by the young girls of the noblest families. On the Parthenon frieze, the joyful procession comes to a halt, not before the ancient temple on the Acropolis, but in an indeterminate place where the gods are gathered together to do honor to their daughter and sister, Athena. It is before this noble assembly that the procession of mortals arrives, with no apparent surprise, and seeming to find quite natural the welcome they receive from the Immortals. Seated around in the most casual attitudes, the joyous Immortals seem to find a real pleasure in receiving the people whom the guest of honor

94 · ATHLETE WITH STRIGIL, FUNERARY STELE (MARBLE). ABOUT 465. DELPHI

95 · YOUNG GIRL RUNNING (MARBLE). ABOUT 480. ELEUSIS MUSEUM

96 · FEMALE STATUE. ACROTERIUM OF THE TEMPLE OF BASSAI. ABOUT 425. LOUVRE MUSEUM. PARIS

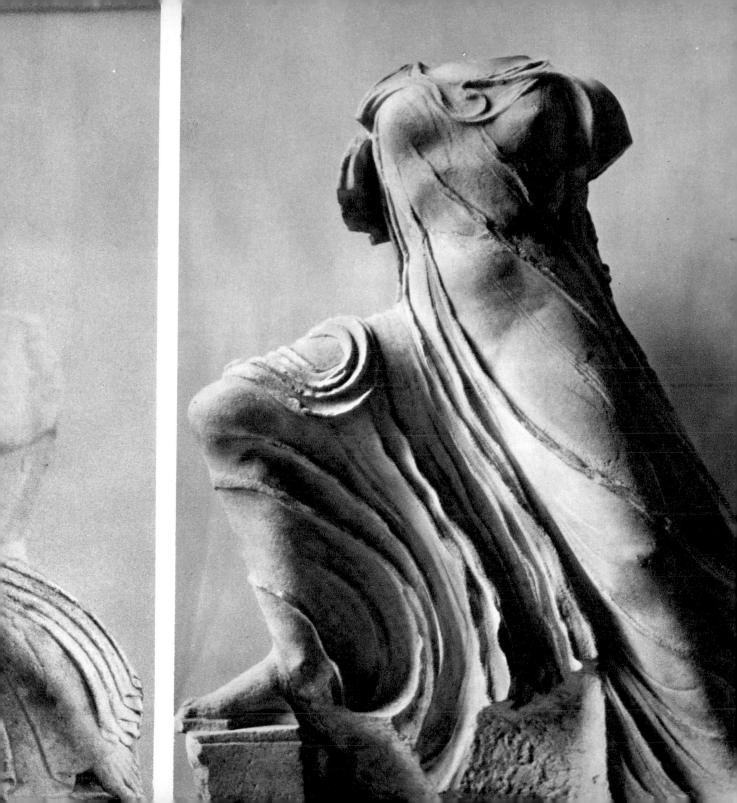

has taken under her protection. To emphasize the fact that it is a family gathering, the tutelary heroes of Attica stand slightly in the background, representing the tradition and the ancestors of the race.

The significance of this long frieze, which is over 170 yards long and includes almost 550 figures of men and animals — the latter being intended for sacrifice — must be sought in the light of Pericles' general policy. If the Athena in gold and ivory is the symbolic personification of Athens, it was necessary too that the people themselves should appear, in their true form, just as they were when the temple was constructed; the allusive significance to be found in, for example, the struggle against the Amazons — because it was Theseus too, so the story ran, who checked their onslaught on Greece — was far too remote. The Parthenon, which to our eyes seems the very image of immortality, was, more than any other Greek monument, an occasional piece, conceived and carried out for the glory of an ideal which was that of the political party then in power.

The pediments too are intended to glorify Athens through her patron goddess. The eastern one depicts the curious legend that tells of the birth of Athena, sprung, motherless, from the head of Zeus, master of the world. It goes without saying that this spontaneous birth conferred on Athena an increase of power which thus benefited those who placed themselves under her protection and were thus, by the same token, under the protection of Zeus. Several of these figures, and unfortunately the most important ones, have been destroyed, but we have some idea of the composition of the scene. In the centre, were represented Zeus sitting on his throne, Athena fully-armed and already full-grown, and Hephaestos, the blacksmith god who, with his hammer, had brought about this strange delivery; in the angles of the tympanum are depicted the principal deities of Olympus to whom Iris, the messenger, was to bring the glad news; those whom she has already passed register amazement, while the rest are still merely waiting. In the two corners, the heads of the horses who drew the chariots of the sun and the moon mark the scene as the dawn of a radiant day....

The western front represented one of the episodes in the life of the goddess which was particularly dear to the hearts of the Athenians. The story was told that Poseidon and Athena had both desired to possess Attica; they had decided to submit the matter to the arbitration of the Athenians themselves, who had chosen Athena in view of her gift of the olive tree. Such was the theme of this pediment: In the centre stood Poseidon, striking the ground with his trident to bring forth the spring which would display his power to the Athenians, but the composition of the whole scene is unknown to us as most of the figures have unfortunately been destroyed.

We can thus see how extensive was the sculptured decoration of this temple. We can see too that the abundance of it was not arbitrary, and that each unit in the decorative scheme had its own part to play in a monument intended to glorify the city by identifying it with its patron goddess.

While it cannot seriously be doubted that Phidias was both director of the works as a whole and also the chief sculptor, it is, however, obvious that he did not himself carry out the sculptured decoration in its entirety. No man could have done it in a single lifetime. Very striking differences

may be recognized in the style of the two friezes, and sometimes even within each one of them, to such an extent that some experts have vainly tried to work out how many artists had been employed on the task, and what was the contribution of each.

The metopes were the first to be executed, and among those that have come down to us, some bear the unmistakable stamp of a traditionalism that is still close to archaism. The Doric frieze, in any case, seems a far less masterly piece of work than that representing the Panathenaea. Admittedly the composition was more often likely to descend to banality by reason of the repeated opposition of Lapith to Centaur, and in spite of the brilliant variations that have been introduced by the artists, this southern frieze is obviously not the best part of the Parthenon sculpture. Greater skill is apparent on the other sides of this Doric order, where the figures are more striking and the attitudes more original. But did each artist compose the slab he was to decorate? It is more reasonable to assume that the sketches had been drawn up by Phidias himself, and that his collaborators had only to carve in marble the figures whose position, attitude, and perhaps the general outline of certain details, were already drawn in on a plan they were to follow.

If, as is likely, Phidias undertook to sculpture a part of the decoration himself, it is no doubt the pediments which, being more exposed to view than the friezes and vaster in scope, must be the work of the master himself. From a study of the two goddesses embracing, who have been identified as Demeter and Core, or else the recumbent figure of Dionysus, we can no doubt get some idea of the master's style. Its outstanding characteristics

97·CHARIOTEER OF DELPHI (BRONZE). 470. DELPHI MUSEUM

are breadth of vision, richness and freedom. There is not the slightest sense of strain, either on the part of the gods represented or on that of the sculptor who created them. The forms are full and vigorous, without exaggeration; the strength of the athletic figures is not openly displayed — it is evident not so much in the swelling of their muscles as in their general aspect, their harmonious proportions that give an impression of power. All the figures move with an ease that creates around them an atmosphere in some sort super-human; one has the feeling that no further problems exist, and that if some difficult question should arise, either for the sculptor or for the figures he has created, it would be solved once and for all by the dictates of reason.

As in all Greek art of this period, there is a certain idealizing tendency which, far from detracting from the impression of life, brings out, in each figure, those aspects which are immediately comprehensible to all mankind, independently of time or race.

98 · PREPARATIONS FOR CHARIOT RACE. EAS

99 · STRUGGLE BETWEEN THE LAPITHS AND

6. WEST PEDIMENT OF THE TEMPLE OF ZEUS (MARBLE). 470/456. OLYMPIA MUSEUM

There was such a vast amount of work to be done on the Acropolis that there must have been very many teams of workmen employed on it. Not only from Athens, but probably from very distant regions, young sculptors came to work under the master. Later they would return to their own country, carrying far and wide the Attic influence by repeating more or less faithfully the processes they had learned in Athens.

But it was not only the hired laborers who flocked to Athens. The fame of the works being undertaken there, and the intellectual atmosphere created by the presence of writers and artists of all kinds in the entourage of Pericles, made Athens such a center of attraction that it practically eclipsed all the other schools that had formerly existed throughout the whole Greek world.

Undoubtedly certain of the masters who were later considered as rivals of Phidias were of Athenian stock, but many too came to learn at the fountain-head, leaving behind their native cities that were lacking in ambition and grandeur. From Crete came Cresilas who was later to make the famous portrait bust of Pericles. From Paros came Agoracritus who was one of the favourite pupils of Phidias, and who was responsible for the colossal statue at Rhamnus in Attica, representing Nemesis, the goddess of Vengeance.

But all these sculptors, such as the Athenian Alcamenes, who seems to have been among the best of them, we know only by tradition, and very little at that. We have to endeavour, through written descriptions left us by ancient writers, to identify anonymous works that Roman copyists have reproduced.

Fortunately, this is not so in the case of one sculptor, Polycleitus, not himself a native of Athens, but one who came there late in life and only infrequently. He was originally from Argos, and, unlike Phidias whose love of experiment is so strikingly obvious through his many innovations, he devoted himself entirely, from his earliest youth, to establishing and reproducing the ideal proportions of the human body — we might almost say, of the male body, for he made very few statues of women, and the only one of which we can form an opinion by considering the copies made of it, is in form and general aspect somewhat masculine. As a theorist, he had laid down the rules which he believed he had discovered, in a didactic work that is unfortunately lost to us, entitled "The Canon," that is, the Rule. We know that he had established as a unit of measure, the thickness of a finger. He had not, however, been content to apply this measurement by arithmetical calculation to the various parts of the body; his calculations were much more flexible, and the very fact that he treated his models in different ways proves that he was continually striving to reach more exact methods of calculation.

His works of sculpture must have been, in his mind, hardly more than an illustration of his theories, and this explains why his different statues were so alike that, as ancient writers pointed out, he had throughout his whole life always reproduced the same model.

He wanted this model to serve as an example to athletes who, by comparing themselves with it, could see the defects in their own bodies and thus correct them. The posture which Poly-

cleitus gave his figures was calculated to facilitate this c
with their legs slightly apart, the weight of the body restin
is more relaxed; the torso is slightly turned from the hip, b
view so that all anatomical details are easily visible; the
else stretched widely apart, extend the chest a
head is either erect or leaning to one side,
importance, for it has no part in the
perform in order to perfect himself; f
inexpressive, and only merits a
unassuming poise.

The work which served a
phorus or Spearbearer. It
athlete, of about the same
fixing on a headband, ha
denoting this action, the D
of an adolescent who is st
shows that Polycleitus' ir
period in the life of man
of a wounded Amazon,
this theme held by the
it was his statue whic
of Phidias and Cresila
with one arm raised
in a such way that her
anatomical detail as tha
The rather massive, or
the Amazon are reminis
The output of Polycle
with that of his contempo
in these male statues merel
kouros type — though admitt
of archaism, and far removed
violent movement. But, from th
figures of athletes were turned
and standing still, which migh
of the male statues of the sixth
prominent place in the history of Gree

ison: they are standing figures,
ne foot only, while the other leg
figure is presented from a front
arms, held close to the body or
ke the shoulders stand out; the
moreover, of merely secondary
ical exercises an athlete must
reason too, it remains singularly
n for its regular features and

cleitus' manifesto was the Dory-
llowed by another statue of an
which, from the fact that he is
n called, from the Greek word
ene. But the less robust figure
early stages of athletic training
ations were not limited to a set
of his most famous statues was
he had entered in a contest on
s of Artemis at Ephesus. And
him the contract, while those
een passed over. The Amazon,
her head, displays her breast
as plainly visible and as rich in
Diadumene or the Doryphorus.
ght say, Dorian proportions of
his other works.
rather limited when compared
Moreover, it is possible to see
st stage of development of the
kouros freed from the restraints
ts early rigidity by its almost
beginning of the fifth century,
quick succession, front view
bly pass for mere derivatives
And yet Polycleitus holds a
ture. Quite apart from the fact

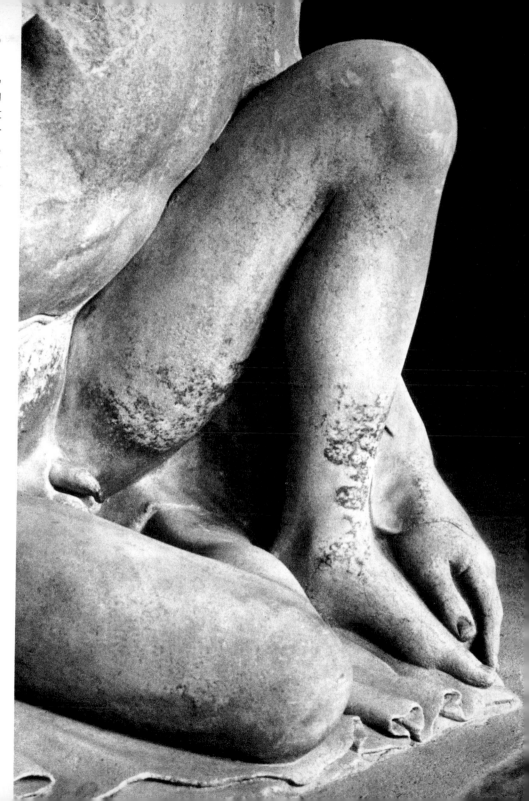

that numerous imitations were made, right up to the Roman period, of the types he had created, either representing some imaginary hero or adding to this idealised body the portrait head of some person who wished to figure as a hero, the works we have cited above embody, more than any others, one of the characteristic trends of Greek thought. "Let no man enter here," a philosopher used to say, "unless he know geometry." While this does not in the least preclude sensibility, the sense of geometry dominated the Hellenic world to a degree unsurpassed anywhere else. Pythagoras is not the only one of the Sages to have attached to the Law of Numbers an importance we have some difficulty in appreciating; we have noted that, right from the beginning, Greek sculptors, though clumsy and often mistaken in their rendering of the details of anatomy, had yet been able to achieve a certain rightness of proportion. Some had favored a fairly elongated type of figure, while others had chosen a rather squat form, but even at the beginning of the sixth century, we rarely find that the relationship between the different parts of the body was not more or less faithfully observed. Is this to be attributed to a quickness of eye on the part of the artist? Or is it not rather that, even at this early date, artists had measured out on a living model the various parts of the body? Measured, and probably systematized. Polycleitus was not the first to conceive the idea of trying to find out the laws governing proportion and giving harmony to the human frame. He undoubtedly took advantage of previous research, and he was certainly well acquainted with all philosophic speculations in regard to Numbers, but he was more able than any other to turn all this to his advantage.

What may surprise us, and with good reason, is the fact that, starting from an established theory, he managed to create works that are astonishingly alive. Nothing is less academic than the living, almost breathing, body of the Doryphorus or the Diadumene, nor more delicately sensitive than the body of the young athlete mentioned above. Geometry serves as a mere basis; it sets the form, and once the structure is established, Polycleitus has been able to give it life — one might also say that his statues are pulsating with life. It was here that the Greek's subtle insight and passion for life came into play, to mitigate the severity of pure logic.

It would be a mistake to attribute Polycleitus' love of geometry to the fact that he was a native of the Peloponnese, for the passion for numbers was common to all Greeks. His Argive origin is apparent rather in his love of athleticism which was passing out of fashion in fifth century Athens, and also in his predilection for massive forms with well-defined contours. While Phidias' work cannot be charged with lack of vigour, yet the power of the gods he created lies, as we have noted above, in the ease with which they move and act. The power of Polycleitus' figures is more human, more of this earth, and less spiritual.

Polycleitus is one of the few sculptors in the latter half of the fifth century who had no real connections with Athens. He was not, however, the only one, and just as the Doric spirit is manifest in his works, so the Ionian school has also its representative who, though not in the class of the

106 · DETAIL FROM THE EAST PEDIMENT OF THE TEMPLE OF ZEUS. HEAD OF A PROPHET

great masters, deserves mention here — a sculptor from Northern Greece, Paionius. He enjoyed quite a wide reputation, for Pausanias, making an obvious error, attributed to him one of the pediments at Olympia. Chance has preserved one of his works, with his signature, a Victory in full flight which was set up on a high triangular pillar and dedicated in the sanctuary of Zeus at Olympia. It is an interesting work, and of undeniable merit, showing a female figure, with far more movement than was usual in works of Pericles' time, with the wind whipping her draperies against her body.

This Victory, which may be dated about 425, is one of the first works which give us an indication of the transformation that was to come about, in the years to follow, in the Greek spirit as in Greek art. Except to a certain extent during the prosperous period when life was easy, at least for some of the people, at the court of the tyrants, the great works of Greek sculpture have always seemed to us to be marked by a certain severity. Religious requirements, the hardships of times when formidable enemies were threatening the country, the grandeur that Pericles sought to bestow on his native city — all these had contributed to give statuary a loftiness of style that was, however, by no means indicative of either conventionalism nor of lack of feeling. The few years of prosperity that Greece had enjoyed before the outbreak of the Peloponnesian War had resulted in a certain relaxing of discipline as it had hitherto existed. People looked more and more to the pleasant side of life; woman was actually, if not legally, emancipated, and was no longer to be considered either as a matron enclosed in the women's quarters, or else as a courtesan whose sole purpose was to provide pleasure for men. Woman's grace of mind was appreciated as much as her grace of body, and coquetry, while not degenerating into licentiousness, took on a new aspect in the manners of women.

This transformation had its repercussions in art, and particularly in sculpture. One has the impression that on the day when Phidias left Athens as the result of a court case brought against him by the enemies of Pericles, a new wave of inspiration swept over Greece which, while not entirely effacing the work and memory of Phidias, at least opened up new possibilities to the sculptor. Confining ourselves to Athens, since right up to the end of the century Athens continued to hold almost a monopoly of monumental works, we have only to compare with the Parthenon friezes or, to take a work of later date, about 420, with the Caryatids which support the upper part of one of the porticos of the Erechtheum, the series of reliefs executed about 410 to decorate a balustrade, erected as a security measure, around the platform on which stood the little temple of Athena Nike, which in modern times has often been called the "Temple of the Winged Victory."

The figures, half life-size, which extend along the full length of this parapet are allegorical figures of Victories occupied in preparing sacrifice to Athena. With their fluid rather than rapid movement, they contrast very strikingly with the austere figures of the young girls taking part in the Panathenaic procession. As on Paionius' statue at Olympia, but even more clearly, the wind whips against their bodies their flowing garments, so transparent that, as when we put on a damp

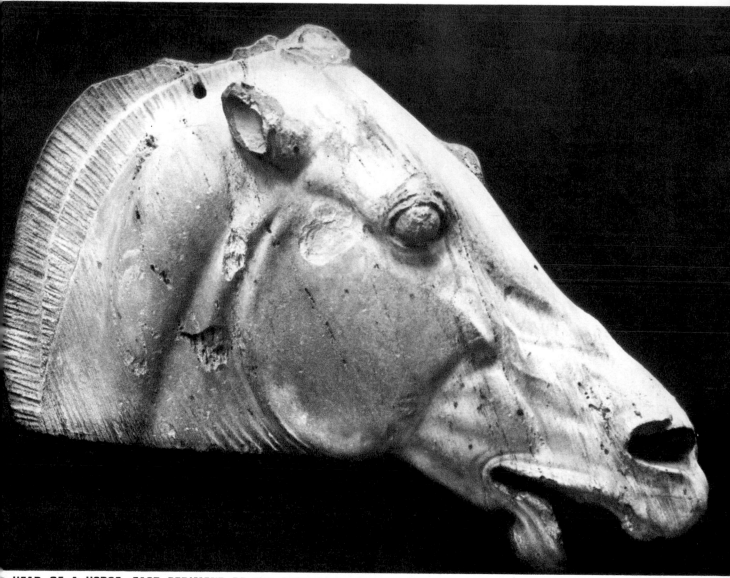

HEAD OF A HORSE. EAST PEDIMENT OF THE PARTHENON. BRITISH MUSEUM. LONDON

material, the slighfest details of anatomy are visible. Although wearing a tunic and a great cape, they appeared as nude, and we may well imagine that the artists who worked on this frieze took a real delight in emphasising the charm, one might even say the seductiveness, of the nude female body. It is quite natural that one of the Victories should lean well forward and bring her knee up high in order to tie up her sandal, but this action has given the artist the opportunity of displaying the roundness of her breasts and the softness of the abdomen. That this tendency was not confined to sculptors, we may see by considering contemporary vase-paintings in which artists took an obvious delight in depicting young women with elaborate hair styles who, because they are engaged in

110 · 111 · BASILE CARRIED OFF BY ECHELOS (MARBLE). LAST QUARTER OF 5TH CENTURY. NATIONAL MUSEUM. ATHENS

making their toilet, prodigally display the mysteries of their body.

This new, or at least newly-avowed, sensuality is but one aspect of the general development of sensibility at this period, and we find in works of the poets, such as Euripides, further proof that this sentiment is vying with the more masculine love of logic that had prevailed in the past. Tenderness, of which we find no trace in sculpture before 450, first appears on the pediments of the Parthenon in the chaste groups bringing together Demeter and Core, Aphrodite and her mother, or, on the west pediment, Cecrops and his daughter. But very rapidly this tenderness was to become less chaste, so that towards the end of the century, in painting at least, eroticism began to appear.

We have not the evidence to know whether, at that time, eroticism found its place in sculpture, for, once the balustrade of the temple of

Athena Nike was completed, the Athenians, overwhelmed by the disasters of the Peloponnesian War, gave up the undertaking of large-scale works for quite a long period. We are not, however wholly without evidence of any kind for the sculpture of the period, for private individuals would order steles for their tombs in order to keep their memory alive.

These steles are very different from those that were turned out in Attica a century earlier, towards the end of the archaic period. They are not even of the same form, being no longer thin slabs of marble greater in height than width, but instead they are now larger and wider slabs leaving more room for the decoration. The transformation is easily explained by the fact that for many years — about three-quarters of a century — the use of these sculptured monuments had been forbidden by a law against luxury, and when this law fell into abeyance about 430, there was no extant tradition constraining artists to conform to an established model.

Precisely because of this change in shape, the motifs represented also underwent transformation. Formerly, the deceased had figured alone on the stele, motionless, photographically fixed in the attitude most apparently representative of his daily life. But now, even when the deceased is figured alone, at least he is less cramped, which seems to enable him to move, as if engaging in some aspect of his former activity. However, he is rarely to be found alone; alongside him stand one or more figures. That these others are men who have died previously and are now receiving him into the realm of the shades, seems not very probable. It is more likely that we have here scenes of parting; with a handshake, which to the Ancients was always a ritual gesture and in general accompanied a religious act, the dying man takes leave of those who survive him, the young wife casts a last glance at her jewel-box, or holds out her arms to the babe she will leave motherless. Tenderness is not entirely lacking in these scenes which, by their very subject, are moving, but never, at least at this period, did artists treat dramatically the theme of everlasting separation; there are no gestures of violent grief, not even a suggestion of pathos. We could easily believe we were looking at a scene from daily life, and that the deceased was about to take a short walk.

While it is not impossible that the scene takes place in the home of the deceased, yet it is more likely to be situated in that unreal world which, on the Parthenon, is the meeting-place of the gods and the Athenians.

These steles, which are the first of a long line of similar monuments, were the work of humble craftsmen; hardly one of them can have been executed by a well-known sculptor, and it has even been considered that those who made them were workmen out of a job when the works begun on the Acropolis by Pericles were discontinued. Being no longer employed by the state, they took orders from private individuals, but with that professional pride and love of beauty that were typical of all Hellenes, they carried on the traditions that Phidias had instilled in them when they had rough-hewn the marble of the metopes under his guidance, and reproduced on the frieze the figures that the master had sketched, and to which he would later put the final touches.

116 · GROUP ON HORSEBACK FROM THE PANATHENAIC PROCESSION (MARBLE). IONIC FRIEZE OF THE PARTHENO

That there was something industrial about the production of these steles is shown by their uniformity; not that we ever find two of them exactly the same, but they are all of the same types seemingly following out models established once for all. And while some of them, such as the stele of Hegeso, are of remarkable beauty, others merely show honest workmanship, but are somewhat lacking in individual character.

Furthermore, these steles had been turned out by a kind of mass production. They were displayed for sale close to the cemeteries, in the masons' workyards, and when the clients had made their choice, it was merely a matter of inscribing the name of the deceased in the space left available above or below the relief. It would therefore be futile to seek any individual likenesses in the figures represented, not only because there is no attempt at portraiture, but in some cases even, the names of the deceased do not correspond exactly to the figures sculptured, some time previously, on the stele.

It must, however, be pointed out that the artists responsible for these works were not always to remain as sober in taste as they had been in the fifth century. First, the steles tended to become really monumental, heavily framed in pillars topped with a false capital; the sculptured plaque is thus further from the eye and the figures are therefore no longer treated in fairly low relief, but almost give the impression of being in the round. At the same time, there are many more of them than before. Around the dead man, or more often the dead woman, crowds the whole family including the servants, and the sorrow of parting, treated with such discretion in former times, was now displayed with greater pathos, with extravagant gestures of grief and heart-rending glances. Such were the last Attic funerary steles when, in 317, an edict of Demetrios of Phaleron forbade the erection of these monuments which vaunted too ostentatiously the petty glories of the wealthy families.

These steles, which range in date over a century, are very valuable evidence for the history of art styles, and the fact that they cover the period almost continuously enables us to follow out the development of taste during this long period.

They are almost the only remaining evidence of Attic sculpture during the dark years immediately following the defeat of Athens in 404, since the city was then so preoccupied with adjusting itself to new conditions that it was forced to forego the undertaking of any major works for the space of at least a generation.

The concluding of a peace treaty in 374 provoked a new wave of optimism in the city, which was marked by the first official contract given out for a long time — a female statue by Cephisodotus representing Peace carrying in her arms the infant Plutos, that is, Wealth. This work marks a major turning-point in the history of Greek sculpture. In the first place, there is its allegorical character. Admittedly, since the time of Hesiod, abstract qualities had been personified, such as Strife, and even more recently Aristophanes had brought on to the stage Demos, the People. A popular motif among vase-painters from the end of the fifth century had been figures bearing the names of Harmony, Desire or Persuasion, but in these cases we get the impression that the figures were drawn first and their names allotted as an after-thought, and that their symbolic value was very limited. It was, however, on the contrary, precisely for its allegorical significance that the Athenians ordered the statue of Peace, and this statue was the first of a long series of figures representing abstract qualities, which were still very popular in Roman times.

But this was not Cephisodotus' only innovation. We have already mentioned how, gradually throughout the latter half of the fifth century, the expression of tenderness was taking hold of art. Never had it been so fully expressed as in the statue of Peace, nor had childhood ever been so glorified. There had certainly been funerary steles representing infants holding out their arms to their mothers, but their rôle was a somewhat accessory one; they were merely there to indicate that the dead woman had been a mother, and, moreover, artists had seldom shown any interest in the appearance of the infants, who were simply represented as minute adults with none of the rounded softness of infancy. Plutos is far from being a perfect figure of a

(MARBLE). YOUNG ATHENIAN WOMEN (ERGASTINES). IONIC FRIEZE OF THE PARTHENON. LOUVRE MUSEUM. PARIS

baby, but Cephisodotus has at least tried to reproduce the typical features of an infant, the large head and chubby limbs. Furthermore, a bond that is spiritual rather than material is apparent between the mother and child, in the gesture of the tiny arms, the forward straining of the child, and the tender glance of the mother. We might also note how the peplum, which draped so severely the Peloponnesian figures of the early fifth century, is here more soft and flowing, in a manner both modest and feminine. In short, this work shows how rapidly Athens recovered from her disasters, and continued to lead the whole of Greece in the field of art.

Although Athens was to lead the way for a long time to come, it was no longer on the Acropolis but in the Peloponnese that, for quite a number of years, the most outstanding works were carried out. Mention must first be made of Epidaurus where the god of healing, Asclepius, who was of comparatively recent origin, had become so popular that his priests felt it necessary to have a more impressive sanctuary built for him. In addition to some large-scale monuments that are not directly concerned with sculpture, they had built a temple which the sculptor Timotheus was engaged to decorate, and he is responsible for the graceful figures at the top of the building, which appear to be taking flight into space. They are either Amazons poised precariously on their mounts, or else figures symbolizing the winds.

A little later, but still before the middle of the century, and again in the Peloponnese, the town of Tegea engaged a young sculptor, Scopas, to draw up plans for a temple to her patron goddess Athena Alea, and to decorate the pediments with sculptures. Scopas, a man from the islands — he was a native of Paros — then began a brilliant career which was to take him later, not only into different parts of Greece as far as Samothrace, but even to the other side of the Aegean Sea, to Halicarnassus and Ephesus. For indeed Greece, impoverished by the almost continuous war of the previous half-century, could no longer supply sufficient work for the artists of the day, who were thus obliged to offer their services to the petty kings of Asia Minor or Syria, who lacked neither the financial resources nor the ambition to rival the Greeks by embellishing their capitals or their palaces.

We have but scant knowledge of Scopas' figures in the round, but considerable fragments of the pediment at Tegea have been brought to light and enable us to form some idea of his style. The very subject chosen for the decoration of the main pediment is one of some pathos; it is the hunting of the Calydonian boar, during which Meleager, taking up the defence of the fair Atalanta, killed his own uncles, thus drawing on himself his mother's curse. We do not know the exact arrangement of the whole design, but we possess isolated heads which are remarkable for the virulence of their expression. It would seem as if, at the very moment when they held the animal at bay, and before the tragedy befell, the hunters could already foresee the fateful consequences of the adventure — that Meleager was to die by the hand of his mother, who preferred his death rather than that he should be overtaken by the Furies whom her own curse had set in his pursuit. They are massive heads, in which the face seems smaller than it actually is, by reason of the dishevelled mass of hair that frames it; the eyes are deep-sunken, under heavy eyebrows, the cheeks drawn and the chin firm, as if man were made to face a destiny that he recognises as impossible

119 · CARYATIDS OF
THE ERECHTHEUM
(MARBLE), ATHENS

to fulfil. We may justifiably imagine that the whole scene was steeped in an atmosphere of violence, and that the bodies were braced and firm, ready to spring to the attack, for, if we are right in attributing to Scopas one of the plaques of the Mausoleum at Hali-carnassus representing an Amazon, her tunic thrown wide open, fighting against the Greeks, we have here exactly the same impression of power and dynamic energy which must have struck those who gazed on the pediments at Tegea.

But of all the works of Scopas, the one that seems to have been most characteristic is the statue of a Maenad carried away by a Bacchic frenzy. This work, described by the writers of Antiquity, was reproduced, and the copy which is now housed in the Dresden Museum gives us a fairly good idea of what the original must have been. In the grip of frenzy, with her body arched like a bow, her head flung back and her hair streaming down behind her, her eyes rolled upwards, and revealed rather than concealed by a tunic held on only by a shoulder strap and a thin cord at the waist, the servant of the God of Extasy was brandishing a kid that she was about to tear apart, as the Maenads actually used to do during those outbursts of mass hysteria that Euripides has described. This

120 · DIONYSUS

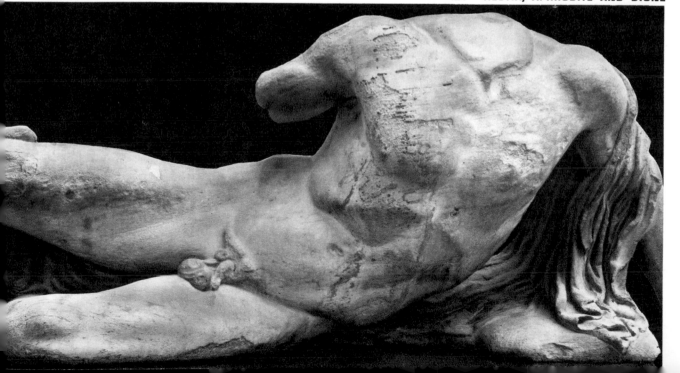

· ILISSOS

121 · HESTIA, APHRODITE AND DIONE

work must belong to about the middle of the fourth century, and it is astonishing to note how far the Greeks had travelled, in less than a hundred years since the death of Phidias, along the road leading from the sublime heights of Reason to the torture-ridden depths of Sentiment and Passion. Some modern writers have spoken of Scopas' romanticism; such comparisons between Antiquity and our own times are often misleading, but it must be admitted that there is something about Scopas' figures that reminds us of the demon-ridden heroes of our own nineteenth century.

Scopas, as we have mentioned, took part in the decoration of a great monument which the Ancients considered as one of the seven wonders of the world, the Mausoleum. This was a gigantic tomb which a prince of Caria, named Mausolus, and his wife Artemis had had erected for themselves on the shores of the Aegean Sea. It was a barbaric monument in many respects: firstly, in its purpose, for the dead were considered as real divinities who were to be worshipped, and secondly, in its appearance, for it was a vast structure, apparently Hellenic in style, but topped by a pyramid. The base supporting the building was decorated with friezes, and it is said that a Greek artist was engaged for the sculptured ornaments of each of the four sides. In addition to Scopas, there was Timotheus, whom we have already mentioned in connection with Epidaurus; Leochares, who is thought to have been the creator of the style of the Belvedere Apollo; and Bryaxis, who is known to us through copies of a majestic Zeux-Serapis. A great number of fragments of these friezes, which have something rather monotonous about them, have been preserved, and it must be admitted that, of them all, the one by Scopas that we mentioned above, is both the most interesting and the finest. It is Scopas who best illustrates how, by deviating from its former reserve, and attempting to make the facial expression correspond to inner thoughts and feelings, fourth century art was yet able to avoid either bombast or maudlin sentimentality.

Halicarnassus was not the only place in Asia Minor where Scopas was engaged. He also worked at Ephesus on the great temple of Artemis. Here, following an Asiatic custom which was never taken up in Greece, the lower portion of certain columns was decorated with reliefs; on one of these columns a scene, which is rather difficult to interpret, showing Hermes the guide of souls, may well be, to judge from the style, the work of the Parian master.

Throughout the diversity of fifth century works, is to be found a common inspiration, and if Phidias, Myron and Polycleitus have little in common, all three of them had at least the desire to render sculpturally what was most noble and admirable in man. Perhaps it is because Reason is one, and imperfection is manifold, that, from the time when art began to interpret sentimentality, sensibility and sensuality, it found a far wider range of expression than in the past.

Between Scopas and another well-known sculptor of his time, there was very little in common. Scopas delighted in rendering the tortures of passion, whereas for Praxiteles it might be said that feeling did not exist at all, only the outward perfection of the human being. Nor was it, in his case, the beauty of the athlete or warrior, but that of the adolescent and of woman. Praxiteles was an Athenian, son of the sculptor Cephisodotus whom we mentioned above, and although we

127 · EAST FRIEZE OF THE PARTHENON: APOLLO. ACROPOLIS MUSEUM. ATHENS

128 · SOUTH FRIEZE OF THE PARTHENON: MEN MAKING SACRIFICE. BRITISH MUSEUM. LONDON

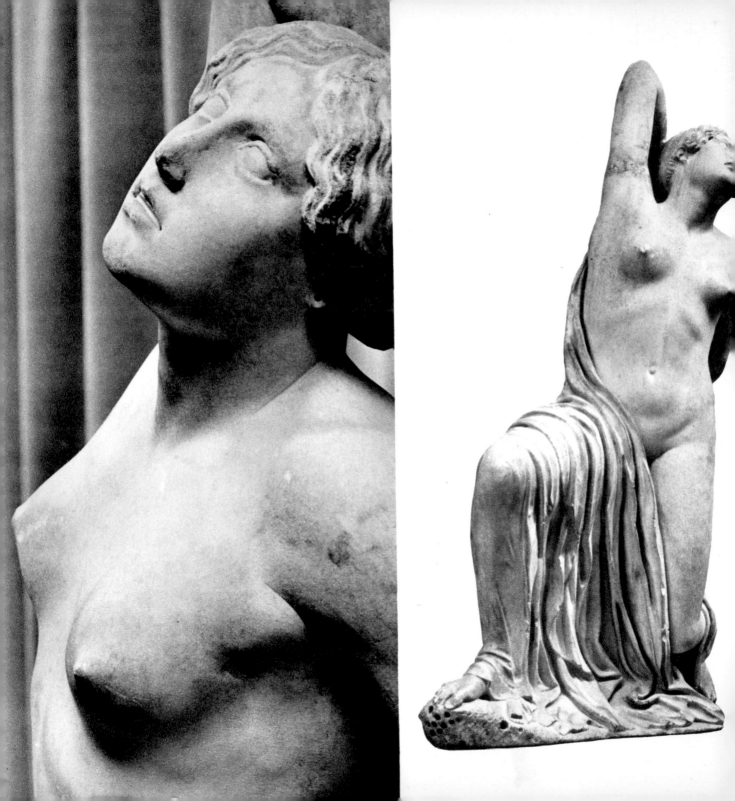

with wine, the Centaurs tried to carry off the bride and her maidens, whereupon a battle took place. But in the eyes of the Greeks, this was not merely a story, and the presence of Apollo himself, set in the center of the pediment to bring peace in the finish and assure the triumph of right over might, shows that this legend had acquired a symbolic value. What we see here is the whole contrast between Barbarism and Civilization. It may be pointed out that this theme had long been a favorite one with the Greeks, and was to be taken up again and again by both painters and sculptors.

It is interesting to reflect that this battle scene is only about thirty years at the most later than that which other sculptors, still steeped in archaism, had represented on the pediments at Aegina. In the temple of Aphaia, as we have seen,

PEDIMENT. WARRIOR

PEDIMENT. HEAD OF ATHENA

PEDIMENT. DYING WARRIOR

PEDIMENT. HEAD OF AND ARCHER

reserved; he is still a very young man, with a rather naive expression, his large eyes wide open and shining with the colored stones that were set in the bronze sockets. His legs are almost tight together, his elbows are pressed against his sides, and his robe, caught in at the waist by a narrow belt, falls in grooved folds which make it seem even longer and give the body the slender sturdiness of a column. His hair, dressed flat against the head and held in place by a headband, is separated into regularly curved locks that seem to accentuate the shape of the head.

Yet for all this, we cannot say that he is motionless. He certainly has both feet firmly planted on the floor of his chariot to brace himself against jolts, not a breath of wind ruffles the stuff of his robe, every muscle in his face is tensed. And yet there is such force, such controlled energy and latent strength in him that his very immobility suggests the possibility, even the desire for movement, the necessity for action. There is something theatrical about the gestures of the tyrannicides, Harmodius and Aristogiton: it is obvious to the spectator that they are lunging in order to strike their enemy, and yet this group, at least if the copies have not misrepresented the original, seems transfixed, as if suddenly paralyzed by some external will. In his total immobility, the Charioteer, by his inner strength, invincibly suggests the idea of movement.

Chance, which has preserved us the Charioteer, has also brought to light another bronze statue of the same period to within a few years. Recovered by some fishermen north of the large island of Euboea, it is probably an image of Zeus, and is now housed in the National Museum of Athens. The god, standing with his legs wide apart, his body turned three-quarters to the side, has his eyes fixed sternly on an adversary at whom he is about to launch a thunderbolt. Here too the impression of movement is extremely striking. One might at first glance be tempted to see in this figure only a variation, though with a very different gesture, of the type from which the Harmodius and Aristogiton group is derived. In both cases, we have figures launching out into violent movement to attack an enemy, the arms are outstretched and the chest fully extended. But whereas the tyrannicides appear to be holding their attitude once and for all, Zeus launching the thunderbolt is, on the contrary, ready to carry through his movement. The artist has stayed him by using the same device as Zeno used to immobilize his arrow, and though we have no impression of over-balancing, at least we can foresee, with the mind's eye, the next phase of the movement which will carry the whole body forward.

This movement, so suggested that we are intensely aware of it, is by no means surprising, for one of the problems most eagerly studied by sculptors between about 475 and 460 was precisely the problem of movement. Many of them were far more ambitious than the anonymous artists of the two bronze statues mentioned above, and the most famous of them, in fact, devoted their energies to representing the human body thrown off-balance by the violence of an untenable and momentary posture.

The name of Myron is known to all, and since ancient times the figure of the Discobolus (or Discus-thrower) has been reproduced many times. An athlete, with his knees bent and body leaning forward, is holding aloft in his right hand a heavy bronze discus that he is about to hurl at the target. Even more than the Zeus that we have just been describing, he is caught in mid-action. It is easy to imagine a live model posing for the Zeus, but nobody could hold, even for an instant, the attitude of the Discobolus. It should therefore not surprise us that the movement is not a real one; a slow-motion film of the whole act of discus-throwing shows that no athlete could ever have combined simultaneously the actually successive attitudes that Myron has here reproduced. This is coming very close to the technique of the archaic period, for with greater knowledge and skill Myron has done what his predecessors had done, incapable as they were of reproducing a movement too rapid for the eye to analyze: he has recomposed the movement in his imagination, and, with greater success than most of the older sculptors, he has left us with the impression that his image is exact. Only photographic tests have made it possible for us to realize that it was not so exact, and perhaps that Myron, with his bold stylization, had been truer than Nature herself.

The Discobolus, which dates from the middle of the fifth century is not one of Myron's earliest works. It is not contemporary with the Zeus nor the Charioteer, but it is the culmination

74 · 75 · SEATED GODDESS (MARBLE).
TARENTUM. ABOUT 480/470. BERLIN MUSEUM

of a whole trend which, even in Myron's
youth, was in full swing. A little older
than Myron was a certain Pythagoras
who had won the admiration of his
contemporaries by his bold treatment
of figures in full movement. And Myron
himself had cast statues in bronze which,
though their movement was less violent,
yet defied the laws of balance. A group
of his used to stand on the Acropolis
at Athens, representing the Silenus
Marsyas trying to get hold of the double
flute which Athena had disdainfully
thrown away. Unfortunately, we do not
know how the two participants in the
scene were placed in relation to each
other, but at least copies of each of them
separately show us that, while the
goddess was in a tranquil pose, just
about to move slowly away from the
spot where she had seen that flute-
playing puffed out her cheeks and
spoiled her profile, the Silenus, on the

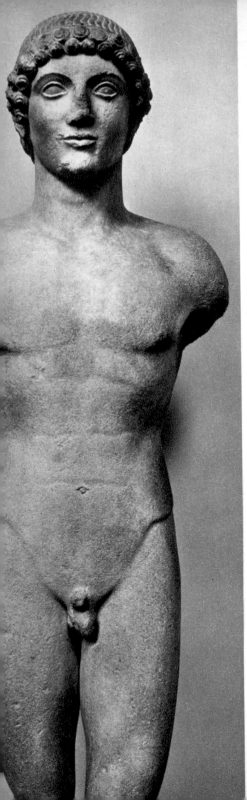

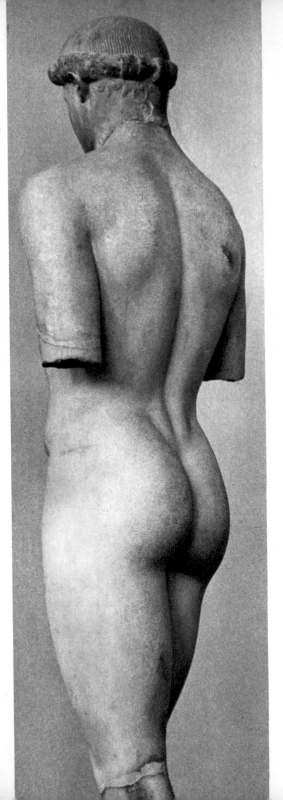

other hand, was figured in
by arching his body and be
of his being caught momen

It would be going too fa
or even for violent movemen
the Greek spirit. Pythagora
from Samos in Ionia, but M
and Boeotia. On the other h
of sculpture which we migh
this tendency at the same
vase-painting of sixth centu
was often carried to the ext
that it was not the Dorians

Among works of Doric
classical period, there is
cannot be overestimated, th
between 470 and 456 at Olyn
which was to contain the
Phidias, was dedicated to
very small area for reliefs,
places: the two pediments a
six on either façade. Betw
contrast that appealed so
sometimes find on either si
and on the other, violent ac

In actual fact, the calr
superficial. The theme ch
temple standing on the site
the preparation for the firs
— the race between the
suitor, the youthful Pelops,

kind of hopping movement which,
ing his legs, gives the impression
ly off-balance.

attribute this desire for animation
one of the two basic currents of
whom we mentioned above, came
was born on the border of Attica
, even if we discount all the works
gitimately consider to be following
iod, we may still note that in the
Athens, the passion for movement
e. It seems probable, in any case,
cultivated it most assiduously.

gin in the years just before the
in particular whose importance
s, the reliefs on the temple erected
in the Peloponnese. This temple,
mous chryselephantine statue by
s. The architect had left only a
gh admittedly in the most striking
in the frieze, twelve metopes only,
the two pediments we find that
gly to the Greeks, and which we
a single vase; on one side, calm,

the eastern pediment is merely
is a very appropriate one for a
ere the Olympic Games were held:
ariot race, the most tragic of all
Oenomaus and his daughter's
whom the Peloponnese took its

ANGFORD APOLLO " (MARBLE). LEMNOS.
ON

OF CRITIOS (MARBLE). ABOUT 480.

POLYCHROME MARBLE) ABOUT 530.

name. The story ran that Oenomaus, having learnt from an oracle that his son-in-law would slay him and take possession of his kingdom, had decided to give his daughter as wife only to the man who could beat him in a chariot race, an impossible feat, as his horses were divine. But Pelops, aided by more powerful gods, won the race, for Oenomaus, thrown out of his chariot, was killed as he struck the ground, and thus the prediction came true.

It was not the race itself that the sculptor depicted. Quite apart from the fact that it is difficult to imagine how a subject of this nature could have been fitted into the framework of the pediment, how much more dramatic it was to show the moment when, the die being cast, the competitors were still ignorant of the outcome. They are alone, moreover, in their ignorance. Zeus, who is presiding over the scene, has already decided; he has placed on his right hand, the lucky side, those whom he wishes to see triumph — Pelops and the young woman he will marry; on his left are those in disfavour—Oenomaus, who has been guilty of many crimes, and who drags his wife Stenope down with him. Also aware of the outcome of the race are the soothsayers who are kneeling in the angles of the pediment, thoughtfully watching the unfolding of the destiny they have already foreseen. It is as if a storm were brooding over the scene, and about to burst. The figures are lined up, one after another, full-face or slightly turned to the side. Even those not directly concerned, like the young slave kneeling in front of one of the chariots, seem to be awaiting some direful event. It is this anguish that appears to be weighing on each one of the figures that gives the whole pediment a sense of brooding disaster, of violence to come.

The west pediment is perhaps, in spite of the fury of the actors in it, more peaceful: it is at least free from the atmosphere of dread. Here the storm has burst, and the outcome, in this case a favorable one, may be foreseen. No dark mystery broods over this scene of one of the most famous combats of Antiquity, that of the Lapithae and the Centaurs. The Lapithae were a peaceful country people, so the legend runs, whose king had invited all his neighbours to his daughter's wedding. Among these neighbours were the Centaurs, monsters half-man half-horse, who lived in the woods by hunting. Flushed

know nothing of his life apart from his liaison with the courtesan Phryne, there is every reason for assuming that he belonged to the refined and fashionable circle of Athenian high society.

Of all sculptors, he was among the few whose fame was most widespread and enduring. Throughout the whole so-called Hellenistic period, the works of Praxiteles were copied and imitated in all materials and all sizes.

His figures were mostly goddesses of grace and charm. The austere Athena had no attraction for him, but of Aphrodite he made many statues. The best-known of them was in the sanctuary at Cnidus, and for the first time, to the great scandal of the pious, the goddess was shown without the slightest drapery. Very often vase-painters had depicted, in scenes which often astonish us by their daring, women entirely devoid of clothing, without this having provoked the slightest scandal, and we even possess some statues of nude women. But in all these cases, mortal women only were concerned; no goddess in her sanctuary had ever been shown naked. Praxiteles had no doubt sought to justify the nudity of Aphrodite by the fact that she was preparing for her bath, and at her feet had been placed a "hydria" or large pitcher containing the water for her ablutions. It was on this pitcher that she had casually thrown down the robe she had been wearing. The pretext is rather a slim one, it must be admitted, and in any case, it was hardly in the act of making their toilet that the gods had previously been displayed to the eyes of the faithful.

Aphrodite is shown as if suddenly surprised by an indiscreet intruder, and she makes some suggestion of modesty by placing one hand before her and the other on her breast. But the fact remains that the statue astonished Praxiteles' contemporaries, and yet, in spite of this, or perhaps even because of it, the statue was soon widely imitated.

Praxiteles also made other statues of the same goddess, and we know, for example, the one which was discovered at Arles, representing Aphrodite half-naked as the veil she was wearing had slipped down as far as her waist.

The figures are well-rounded, but the proportions seem finer and less heavy than in the past. The head is small and narrow, with regular facial features, and whereas in former times the hair was plastered against the head thus outlining the shape of it, we now find that, following a fashion that women seem to have adopted about the end of the fifth century, hair-styles are far more elaborate, with high chignons which, sometimes on the top of the head but more often on the nape of the neck, catch in a heavy mass of ringlets that had already been crossed over the temples; they were set off by diadems and ribbons, and from this time on hair-styles came into their own, and were no longer a mere outline of the head.

The facial expression is very different from that which Scopas gave his figures. The figures of Praxiteles are as calm as those of Scopas are passionate. They have neither the majestic serenity of Phidias' creations, nor the impassivity of Polycleitus'; the smallness of the eyes and the thin lips give them a somewhat cautious and slightly malicious expression. They are

DETAILS FROM THE FRIEZE
DECORATING THE BALUSTRADE
OF THE TERRACE OF THE
TEMPLE OF ATHENA NIKE
(MARBLE). ABOUT 410.
ACROPOLIS MUSEUM. ATHENS

131 · VICTORY UNTYING HER
SANDAL

133 · WINGED VICTORY

132 · ATHENA IN FRONT OF
THE BOUNDARY-POST OF THE
STADIUM (MARBLE). ABOUT 450.
ACROPOLIS MUSEUM. ATHENS

134 · NEREID OF EPIDAUROS
(MARBLE). WEST FAÇADE OF THE
TEMPLE OF ASCLEPIOS. ABOUT 370.
NATIONAL MUSEUM. ATHENS.

divinities that have no gentleness; Aphrodite takes delight in making her devotees suffer, while her son Eros, whom Praxiteles frequently represented, carries his bow and arrows for wounding the hearts of mankind.

But Aphrodite and Eros are not the only Immortals treated by Praxiteles. Artemis also inspired him, perhaps because she too was a cruel goddess. She is figured as a young girl, scantily clad, slim and rather boyish with her sinewy and somewhat unfeminine grace. As the counterpart of this statue (which is known as the Diana of Gabii), her brother Apollo is shown leaning against a tree on which a lizard is climbing. He is going to kill it, for, according to legend, Apollo Sauroctonos was the destroyer of reptiles and sauria, but for the moment he seems rather to be playing with it, and the scene has the somewhat sentimental appeal that we find in curios. The very appearance of the god is charming rather than impressive; while his sister has something boyish about her, Apollo, on the other hand, with his widish hips, slender limbs and long hair, may well seem rather too feminine; we may recall that a hermaphrodite is mentioned in the catalogue of Praxiteles' works.

Neither Scopas nor Praxiteles sculptured any but mythological characters, with the result that the face is necessarily idealized, and presents no individual character. And this is a fact worthy of note, for at the time when these artists lived, a new genre had already come into favor; it may even be said that the fourth century was the age of portraiture. It will be remembered that, as we have mentioned above, Cresilas, a century earlier, had made a portrait of Pericles, and other portraits of the same period might also be quoted. But these portraits all had one thing in common — the artists had set out to stylize the model, to see the man, not as an individual, but as representative of a particular social class. This was no longer the case in the fourth century. Perhaps the development of individualism had something to do with it; perhaps too, the Greeks were influenced by their increasing contact, in the late fifth and early fourth centuries, with the petty kings of the East who set themselves up as gods, and had statues made in their likeness. The fact remains that, as early as 450, the custom had grown up in Greece of dedicating statues of persons who had won fame in some field or other; poets, philosophers, statesmen were considered worthy of having their portraits done in marble and set up in a sanctuary or some public place.

The enthusiasm for portraiture was carried to such lengths that artists even went so far as to make imaginary portraits, of persons long since dead, or even of half-legendary heroes such as Homer, though it was quite obvious that such portraits could not reproduce a true facial likeness.

The not unlikely theory has been put forward that the habit of certain rulers of having their likeness struck on coins played a considerable part in the development of the art of portraiture. This art was, in fact, later to develop even more extensively than in the fourth century, during the breaking up of Alexander's empire into separate kingdoms, in which each prince and his entourage were anxious to perpetuate their memory by bequeathing their portraits to posterity. However, it was even before the conquest of Greece by Macedonia that portraiture had become widely popular. It was never to become as crudely realistic as among the Romans, for we can recognise the Greek artists' desire to seek out in their models whatever was common to mankind in general rather than to the particular individual in question, yet all the same it has been possible to identify persons of this period by means of written descriptions, which is fair proof of the personal character of the works concerned.

Some very great artists confined themselves solely to this form of art, but it was also practised intermittently by sculptors who worked in all genres. Lysippus in particular comes to mind, a sculptor who holds a somewhat special place among artists of the fourth century. He came from the Peloponnese, and perhaps for this reason remained faithful to the athletic ideal that had been scorned by Praxiteles but favoured by Polycleitus. Yet there was a world of difference

136 · FUNERARY STELE OF MNESARETE, DETAIL (MARBLE). ATTICA. EARLY 4TH CENTURY. GLYPTOTHEK OF MUNICH

between the outlook of Lysippus and that of Polycleitus. While the older master had limited himself to the representation of a single model, and had denied his statues movement so that the muscle and bodily structure of the athlete could be better studied than if they had been deformed by any violent action, Lysippus, on the other hand, set out to portray ephemeral aspects of the body, even when it is almost motionless. The most famous work of Lysippus shows a man standing naked, scraping the dust off himself, after finishing his physical exercise, with a sort ot curry-comb called a strigil; the arm he is cleaning is stretched forward, thus expanding the torso, his legs are straight and firm, and his head erect, his eyes looking into space. It is in no way comparable with Myron's art; no violent movement agitates the Apoxyomene (the Greek word denoting one who scrapes himself with a strigil), and we are not in the least tempted, as with the Discobolus, to carry through his movement with the mind's eye. Above all, the figure is perfectly balanced; there is no impression of instability to give the illusion of an arrested action.

Illusion plays a considerable part in the work of Lysippus. He was one of the first, if not the first, to realise that the division of the body into front view, side view and back view, is purely arbitrary, that the planes are not clear-cut, and that the eye follows with a continuous movement the curve of the hip towards the chest, or from the back of the head to the neck. A statue by Polycleitus could be viewed from the front, the side or the back, but it was not so made as to be viewed from the intermediary angles. Perhaps it was the play of light, the contrasting effects between shade and the gleam of bronze — for Lysippus was a worker in bronze — that gave spectators this illusion, but the fact remains that a statue by Lysippus could be viewed from any angle without detriment to the composition as a whole.

Lysippus found both fame and personal satisfaction in this invention, which was surely his, and it was no doubt he who sculptured the statue mistakenly called Jason. It is, in actual fact, the messenger god Hermes, fixing on his sandal, and he is shown simultaneously from front, back and side. Though leaning forward, he is turning the upper part of his torso to the left, which gives his body a flowing indeterminate line that makes it seem, though actually motionless, to be vibrant with movement.

At the same time, to add to this impression of quivering life, Lysippus elongated the proportions fixed by his predecessors. The standard figure of Polycleitus was somewhat on the thick-set side, while that of Lysippus was rather tall and slender, while the relationship of the head to the body was decreased from one-sixth to one-seventh. Whether this innovation be attributed to him, as ancient writers claimed, or not, we have already noted that the figures of Praxiteles were tending to greater slimness than those of the previous century, with their small head on a very long neck. And from other instances too, it may be seen that the tendency to elongate forms was characteristic of the fourth century as a whole. Even vases, at this time, were becoming more slender in form.

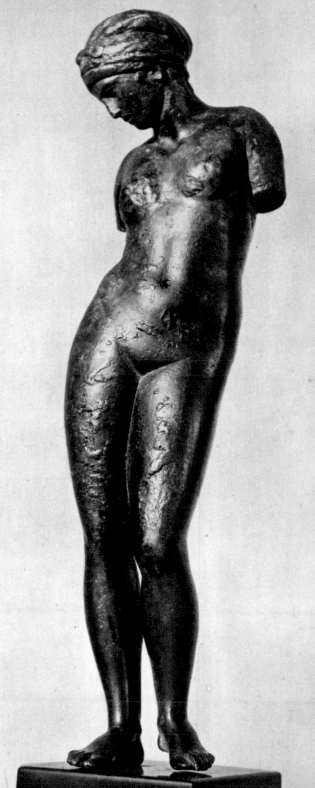

139 · SCENE, PROBABLY OF UNDERWORLD (MARBLE). SCULPTURED BASE OF A COLUMN OF THE TEMPLE OF ARTEMIS AT EPHESUS. ABOUT 340. BRITISH MUSEUM. LONDON

We shall not discuss the other statues of Lysippus; whether it was the master himself, or one of his close disciples, who sculptured for the sanctuary at Delphi an Agias that was part of a votive offering from Thessaly, is of small importance here. But we know that Lysippus was the only sculptor whom Alexander, who had a great affection for him, authorized to reproduce his likeness. And among the numerous portrait busts of the great conqueror — some of them rather severe, others, made after the king's death, as romantic as one could wish, with languorous eyes and flowing locks tossed in the wind — there is one which we know from copies, especially from a bust in the Louvre called Alexander Azara, which, with its wiry vigour, intelligent features and keen eyes, bears the stamp of a great master. Might it not be precisely one of the better copies of a work by Lysippus?

THE HELLENISTIC PERIOD

Lysippus still belonged to what has been generally called the classical period. The conquests of Alexander, the advance of Greek armies and Greek administration from the Aegean Sea to the shores of the Indus and to the lower cataracts of the Nile, marks an important transformation in the history of Hellenism. The city-state, which up to that time had been the sole political unit, was now no more than a geographical entity within an organised kingdom; the will of the citizens prevailed only in municipal affairs, and higher authorities wielded power over extensive regions. When Alexander's generals divided up their master's empire, Greece was but a small province in that vast area which has been called the Hellenistic world.

But this transformation perhaps affected art less than all other aspects of life. Even at the beginning of the fourth century at the latest, trade exchanges, travel, and orders from abroad, had brought Greek artists in touch with eastern civilization; princes of Sidon had called over Greek sculptors to decorate their sarcophagi, the kings of Lycia in Asia Minor had had monuments erected in their capital in imitation of those on the Acropolis, and the fact that the Persian Empire had now fallen into the hands of Greek generals had the result that Greek sculptors, whom their own country was no longer able to employ, were in greater demand than ever.

The market for their activity was, in fact, immense. Not only the kings themselves, but their whole entourage of officers, courtiers and business-men, the whole crowd of newly-rich that had been attracted to countries of such potential wealth, desired to be considered as persons of culture and refinement, and consequently ordered from Greek artists works to beautify their

142 · HEAD OF A YOUNG GIRL (MARBLE). CHIOS. LATE 4TH CENTURY. BOSTON MUSEUM
143 · HEAD OF DEMETER (MARBLE). CNIDUS. 2ND HALF OF 4TH CENTURY. BRITISH MUSEUM. LONDON

homes and gardens. Enormously wealthy private individuals took over from the impoverished Greek cities.

It must not, however, be imagined that art, at any rate in the beginning, benefited greatly from this sudden surge of activity. If the artists were to become rich, at least they had to satisfy the taste of their customers who, full of a somewhat blind admiration for the greatest works that Greece had produced, imposed on the artists a narrow academic style. It was the great ambition of everyone to have at least a copy of the masterpieces at Athens and Delphi. The originality of the Hellenistic period in the field of art has often been overemphasized, and we are inclined to forget that this kind of inventiveness is of a very particular type, and that from beginning to end the Hellenistic period was an age of insipid classicism, devoid of spontaneity. This is not to say, however, that no masterpieces were created, even in this academic genre. We shall not discuss here the aesthetic value of the Venus de Milo; it is equally undeniable, both that the work has always had, and always will have, a wide popularity, and also that it is very strongly inspired by the creations of Praxiteles.

Praxiteles was, in fact, the sculptor whose works were most highly prized, and, as we mentioned above, copies were made by the thousand of his Aphrodites, especially that of Cnidus, even in the most remote provinces of Alexander's empire. They were the ancient equivalent of decorative mantlepieces: the statues were placed in little niches hollowed out in the walls to house cult images, they were set up in sanctuaries for the adoration of the faithful, and

144 · 145 · THESSALIAN VOTIVE OFFERINGS (MARBLE). MIDDLE OF 4TH CENTURY. DELPHI

the sensual character of this art only added to its popularity.

The other sculptor of the classical period who remained in fashion was, strangely enough, Polycleitus. On his nude and generously proportioned bodies of athletes, civil servants who were, no doubt, less athletic in appearance, would have their own portrait head placed, and have the whole statue set up in the public square of their village, thus displaying themselves in the nudity that had become the symbol of elevation to the status of hero. In Polycleitus conception of man, there was a certain strength, gravity and nobility that doubtless appealed very strongly to the newly-rich of the Hellenistic period, and, on the other hand, we may imagine that sculptors were not ill-pleased to reproduce statues they must have copied many a time during their apprenticeship.

Among more refined spirits, admiration for the past found a more subtle expression. Throughout the classical period, archaic works had been, if not completely unknown, since a number of sixth century monuments or even earlier ones had been left standing, at least heartily despised. At a time when artists were conscious of their technical mastery, and were capable of expressing almost anything they wished, the fumbling attempts of their distant predecessors seemed to them grievous errors, and only

6 · 147 · YOUNG MAN (BRONZE). DISCOVERED IN THE A NEAR ANTICYTHERES (SOUTH OF THE PELOPONNESE). D HALF OF 4TH CENTURY. NATIONAL MUSEUM ATHENS

148 · HEAD OF MAUSOLUS (MARBLE). HALICARNASSOS. AB

149 · HEAD OF A WOMAN (BRONZE). SATALA (ARMENIA).

150 · HEAD OF A BOXER (BRONZE). OLYMPIA. LATE 4TH CE

151 · HEAD OF HYGIA (MARBLE). TEGEA. MIDDLE OF 4TH C

BRITISH MUSEUM. LONDON

CENTURY. BRITISH MUSEUM. LONDON

NATIONAL MUSEUM. ATHENS

NATIONAL MUSEUM. ATHENS

those whose piety was bound up with tradition remained aesthetically faithful to the ancient idols that were still adored in the sanctuaries.

During the Hellenistic period, a certain number of enlightened amateurs, perhaps a trifle wearied by the popularization of the classical ideal, began to reconsider the works of former times and to appreciate their charm. Numerous attempts were made, as we shall see further on, to bring new life into an art that was becoming decadent, and some artists sought to bring about this rejuvenation by a return to the simplicity of earlier times. Immediately amateurs began to vie with each other for the purchase of the very few archaic works to be found on the market, while artists, on their part, set themselves to imitate these works, fully confident that, in reproducing certain processes of the older masters, they would thereby convey that impression of artlessness that marked the kouroi and the kores. A whole new school sprang up, favoring the return to archaism. The works it produced are not all lacking in merit or charm, but their main interest lies in the fact that they show clearly that artlessness cannot be imitated, and that spontaneity can never be acquired by effort.

But academism and a blind devotion to recognized masterpieces are fortunately not the only aspects of Hellenistic art. One of the more fortunate results of Greek expansion across Asia and Egypt was the establishing of closer ties between peoples than in the past. This aspect must not, of course, be exaggerated; the arrival of a few thousand Greeks in Anatolia or the Nile Valley did not change the general character of the common people. But among the enlightened classes, a certain amount of fusion took place, which had a direct influence on artistic creativeness, most particularly on its general conception, for the Greeks had carried technical skill to such a pitch that it was almost always in a Greek medium that even foreign ideas were expressed.

Admittedly, while a common mode of expression established a kind of uniformity among the productions of the various regions, yet, in the study of the Hellenistic period, a certain number of sectors, and considerable ones at that, must be distinguished — schools in which the local outlook left its particular stamp.

Among these schools, one whose influence was most brilliant and far-reaching was situated in a city founded by Alexander, and which very rapidly became one of the capital cities of the world, Alexandria. The dynasty of the Ptolemies who ruled over it was distinguished from the start by its patronage of arts and letters. Unfortunately, though the school of poetry which developed there shows certain marked characteristics, it is more difficult to distinguish the purely Alexandrian element in the general artistic production of the Hellenistic world.

Naturally no doubt is possible in the case of a series of reliefs depicting scenes peculiar to Egypt and the Nile Valley landscape. On the base of a statue representing, in the recumbent figure of a majestic old man, the river to which Egypt owed her prosperity, a whole series of little pictures was sculptured, showing crocodiles, elephants and palm trees; only at Alexandria would

such a representation be explicable. But the problem becomes far more difficult when we come to consider the so-called "pictorial reliefs."

These reliefs are typically Hellenistic. They give Nature and landscape — both urban and rural — a place that would have been unthinkable in the classical age. For the Greeks of the earlier period had been concerned solely with man, and they had introduced a scenic decor only when this was absolutely essential for the understanding of the subject in question. And even in these cases, they stylized the background as far as possible, with no concern for realistic treatment; a dried tree-trunk or a rock, as visibly artificial as stage scenery — this was all that landscape meant before the Hellenistic period. But the peoples with whom Alexander's armies had come into contact were, on the contrary, accustomed to look upon man as of small importance in the general scheme of things, and to feel that he was insignificant in comparison with Nature. As they were country rather than city people, they were sincerely attached to the countryside around them; their divinities were bound up, even more than those of the Greeks, with the mountains and forests and the land itself. Art felt the impact of this foreign outlook, and whether it be that sculptors and painters living outside Greece proper, in the newly-conquered territories, adopted the tastes of the people among whom they were living, or whether they simply adapted themselves to the wishes of their clients, they took great care to observe the background against which the scenes they depicted took place. It might even be said that in many cases the landscape was treated for its own sake, and that the persons depicted in it were merely incidental.

Is it therefore to be assumed, from the fact that some of these landscapes are typical of the Nile Valley, that this new love of Nature among the Greeks

153 · 154 · HERMES OF PRAXITELES CARRYING THE INFANT DIONYSOS, HIS BROTHER (MARBLE). ABOUT 330 . OLYMPIA MUSEUM.

had its origin in Egypt? Or, when we see a hunter shaking a dead hare in front of his dog's eyes, in the shade of a plane tree, might we not be tempted to conclude that this predilection for natural landscape arose in the forests of Asia Minor? It may even be possible that, independently of one another, artists facing similar requirements on the part of their clients, practised each on his own account a genre that was not very difficult to create.

If the Alexandrian origin of the pictorial relief is not absolutely certain, it appears probable, on the other hand, that the development of a taste for realism, sometimes carried to the point of caricature, may be ascribed to Egypt. Since very early times, the humor of the Egyptian fellahin had found an outlet in artlessly cruel drawings of the misfortunes that fell to their lot, and the caustic wit of the Pharaohs' subjects was well known. The arrival of the Greek conquerors did not change this general tendency; old women, with wrinkled faces, sometimes holding the bottle from which they had drunk rather too copiously, grotesque dancing girls, humble people bowed down by the weight of their existence — these are the themes that recur most frequently, as much in the bronzes and terra cottas as in the statues of the Alexandrians. It may well be asked for what purpose these works were created, as they can hardly have been made for dedication in a sanctuary. They were made solely to please the eye, and for the amusement of their owners. Genre sculpture had come into being.

To genre sculpture we may also, no doubt, attribute many of those pseudo-classical works of all sizes which were so highly prized in Alexandria even more than in the rest of the Hellenistic world, the nature of which we sought to define earlier in this chapter.

Another city, as noteworthy in the field of art as Alexandria itself, was Pergamum. Situated inland in the north-west of Asia Minor, Pergamum did not owe her prosperity to commerce as did the Egyptian metropolis, but the intelligent and unscrupulous enterprise of her rulers had brought her into the limelight. Even before the end of the third century, large-scale works had been carried out there. About 228, in the temple that had been dedicated to Athena, King Attalus I had a votive offering set up to commemorate his victories over the Gauls whose invasions had threatened his country, and a few years later he dedicated, not in his capital but in Athens, a whole series of statues recalling the wars he had undertaken. These votive offerings were, as far as we can judge from copies, similar in more than one respect.

The most striking feature of these works is their pathos; they represent fallen enemies, mortally wounded. In some cases, in a rather theatrical manner, they seem to be defying the fate that awaits them; in other cases, they are completely stricken, sinking down with half-closed eyes and an expression of intense suffering on their faces. These figures were, in fact, to serve as models for countless imitations, and vanquished Gauls became a favorite subject at that period. But pathos is not the only notable aspect of these statues. Interest in what we call local color, an interest which had for a long time not existed at all but which had made a hesitant appearance towards the end of the fifth century, found its fullest expression in these works. Attalus wanted

wished to draw up an exact chronicle of their exploits. The votive offerings of Attalus belong to that historical sculpture which the Greeks, with their love of generalization, had always so scrupulously avoided. Attalus, in this respect a precursor of the Romans, took every care that no misunderstanding should arise on the subject of his exploits, and the artists engaged by him were to render an exact account of what he had accomplished.

These two votive offerings at Pergamum and Athens, for all their intrinsic interest, are, however, not by any means as valuable, to our eyes, as the most famous work of the Pergamene school, the sculptured frieze of the great altar which Eumenes 11 dedicated to Zeus and Athena on the acropolis of his capital.

This altar, which was of colossal size, had an almost square base, on the southern side of which was a stairway leading to the platform. The total perimeter of this base was occupied by a continuous frieze over 370 feet long, representing, in figures of greater than human size, the Battle of the Gods and Giants. The idea of decorating vast wall surfaces was not a new one, and the Persians, after many others, had used it on the Palace of Darius at Persepolis. There had been other instances of sculpture covering the base of monuments, such as the so-called Nereid monument at Xanthos, which was in reality the tomb of a Lycian prince, and on the Mausoleum at Halicarnassus. But in Greek art properly so-called, there is no point of comparison. Moreover, neither in Lycia nor at Halicarnassus, was the area covered by friezes so vast.

The theme itself was not, in its conception, particularly original. On vases, and on the pediments and friezes of many temples, since the beginning of Hellenism, artists had delighted to celebrate the victory which had won for the Olympians their universal supremacy. But, except in rare instances, all of which belong to the archaic period, the struggle between the two sides had always appeared as a battle between human beings. The Giants had certainly been given a somewhat savage appearance, but they were not monstrous, and we may see in this fact a proof of the general abhorrence of the Greeks for all that was not consonant with human reason. At Pergamum, on the contrary, in a wild and pitiless mêlée, we see the clash of the gods, who at least were represented in accordance with tradition, with beings created, out of all human proportion, by the exuberant imagination of the East — figures the like of which had not been seen since primitive sculptors, more or less copying Eastern models, had sculptured for temple pediments creatures with human head and torso, but ending in a serpent's tail. Wild animals take part in the battle, and the Giants have such a violent and tortured expression that their faces are barely human at all. Their mouths are wide open as they shout, their eyes dart lightning from under shaggy eyebrows, their muscles are contracted, and the whole battle mêlée is on an epic scale that lifts it above the mode of normal combat.

The forced, theatrical aspect of the figures is no doubt due to the fact that, although the frieze was ordered by a Greek prince, it was sculptured in a barbarian atmosphere — barbarian in the ancient sense of the word, i.e. outside the Hellenic world. The declamatory side of this composition

has been much criticized, f
gestures, its wild display of
intensity of suffering heig
lamentation of the Giants.
certain grandeur in this ver
the whole work is vibrant wit
ement, unbridled it is true,
powerful, and the group com
the Giant Encelades, and Ge
ing for the life of her child,
compared with the fine gro
the Arch of Triumph.

The strikingly dramatic c
frieze appears as one of the
of the art of this school, and
Asia Minor as a whole at th
Pergamum that is thought to
place of origin of that moving s
hanging by his hands from a
flayed alive by order of Ap
is thin and sinewy, as might
a wild creature of the forest,
anguish twists the drawn fac

It is a curious thing that
of Pergamum, where violenc
exaggeration of form were
was also the place of origin
most delicate works created
lines, in which artists, as we m
strove to add to the appeal c
itions with just a touch of arch
a mere fragment of a larger de

its dramatic
ce, and the
ed by the
there is a
xaggeration;
fe and mov-
t extremely
sing Athena,
Earth plead-
often been
by Rude on

acter of this
inctive traits
haps even of
period. It is
ve been the
e of Marsyas
trunk to be
The body
expected in
a spasm of

same city
feeling and
emphasized,
some of the
traditional
oned above,
eir compos-
; one relief,
represents

EMETRIUS 1.
). MIDDLE OF
SEUM. ROME

S (BRONZE).
EUM. ATHENS

a dancing girl shrouded in her veils, and the charm of the work calls to mind the graceful statuettes of Myrina.

Alexandria and Pergamum were not the only schools of sculpture; apart from art centers of secondary importance, in which sculptors were no doubt content to imitate the production of the greater schools, mention must be made of the school of Syria. It was not one of the more original schools, and artists there seem to have been content to reproduce, in rather more rounded form, the models created by Praxiteles and his fellow-artists.

Of greater interest is the school of Rhodes, whose masterpiece is undoubtedly that great image of Victory which was, probably during the second century, dedicated on the island of Samothrace. Set up on the prow of a galley, this Victory, with the wind lifting her draperies or whipping them tight against her, is one of the boldest and most successful representations, in the whole of Greek antiquity, of a magnificent body battling against the elements.

It would no doubt be possible to distinguish even more precisely the influence and the characteristics of the art of each particular region. And yet it must be admitted that, if Greek was the only medium of expression from the Adriatic to the Lebanon, the same may be said of art, for which reason it is very difficult, for a period in which the same styles were in vogue in Tyre as in Athens, to distinguish local trends as in the archaic period, and thus to be able to discern the place of origin of various statues.

The fact that a common ideal existed is proved by the general popularity of the portrait. We have already pointed out how this genre had come into fashion in the fourth century, but it was during the Hellenistic period that its popularity became most widespread. Portraits became increasingly realistic, and as time went on, the individual character of the model who posed for the artist stood out more and more distinctly. There is still a certain degree of idealization, in that the sculptor concentrates on those features which seem to him the most typical and interesting; he does not reproduce everything, nor encumber his composition with a mass of insignificant detail that would detract from the desired effect, but the details he has accentuated enable us to recreate the image of a living person. Each local school treated the portrait in accordance with a certain technique and a spirit that characterized its whole production, and thus we find a more gentle note in an Alexandrian portrait than in one sculptured in Asia Minor. But they are closer to each other than either of them is to a Roman portrait.

It would be quite arbitrary to assess an even approximate date by which Greek sculpture had ceased to exist. It is considered by some that the Hellenistic period came to an end at the time when what had been Greece came under the political power of the Romans. But while the new regime and foreign domination had historical consequences whose importance cannot be too greatly stressed, one may say that they had no influence on the development of art, for, since Macedonian hegemony had put an end to the autonomous city-states, and great kingdoms had been set up, sculptors had always worked for rulers or for wealthy private individuals. Whether

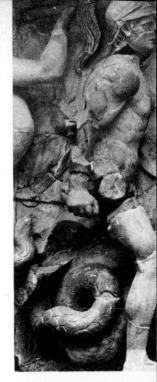

his votive offering to be perfectly understood by all; his different victories were all to be commemorated, and consequently the adversaries he had encountered were to be clearly distinguished. Thus the representatives of each people were made recognizable not only by their costume, but also by their physical appearance. The Gauls, who were a semi-barbarous people, are represented naked, wearing only round their necks the heavy Celtic collar called the torque; they are tall and broad-shouldered, their facial features lack any trace of refinement, and their masses of tangled hair, which seem never to have been combed, fall in long locks over their forehead and down their back. The Persians wear not only the clinging garment which Greek art had always faithfully reproduced, but even their wide faces and prominent cheek-bones proclaim them immediately as of a foreign race. We can see in this a tendency which had never been an aspect of Hellenism; this desire for racial identification was more than a desire for the superficially exotic. In the manner of Oriental rulers, from the remote Sumerian period to the closer period of the Assyrians, war leaders in Asia had always

65 · APHRODITE CROUCHING (MARBLE). LATE 2ND CENTURY. ARCHAEOLOGICAL MUSEUM. RHODES

66 · JOCKEY (BRONZE). 2ND CENTURY, DISCOVERED IN THE SEA NEAR EUBOEA. NATIONAL MUSEUM. ATHENS

67 · BOXER AT REST (BRONZE). MIDDLE OF 1ST CENTURY. NATIONAL MUSEUM. ROME

these masters had a Greek or a Roman name was of small importance, especially as the conquerors were quite prepared to steep themselves in a civilization they judged superior to their own, and had no desire to impose their personal tastes on the artists whom they employed.   As for the Roman citizens who came to settle as tradesmen or civil servants in countries that were formerly Greek, these did not impose on the artists who worked for them conditions in any way different from those imposed by the Syrians, Egyptians or Persians who had been incorporated into the empire through Alexander's conquests.   Greek art survived, therefore, faithful to its lineage, right through to the time when barbarian peoples overcame the power of Rome, and when the various races of the Empire ceased to obey the central power of the Emperor and began to live, somewhat precariously, their own national lives.

Greek art extends, therefore, over a period of more than a thousand years. While sculpture was not the earliest manifestation of this art, it made its appearance at least as early as the seventh century, and its popularity, which was great even in its beginnings, grew more and more as people began to develop enthusiasm for plastic art.   During this long career, Greek sculpture produced works of many different types, and it is quite natural that men of modern times, in accordance with prevailing fashion, should admire now one period, now another.   If, in the present volume, Hellenistic sculpture has been treated rather summarily, it is because our own times have tended to disregard it, perhaps somewhat unjustly.

But from the viewpoint of the historian, who sets out to explain the works themselves, and to determine their origin, no period is of less interest than any other.   Aesthetic considerations are not involved; what matters is to place the work in its proper context and to trace the general lines of development.   Now, with remarkable continuity, and complete fidelity to an ideal, Greek sculpture aimed from first to last, not at reproducing a photographic likeness of a particular model, but at creating, in statue or bas-relief, an impression of life.   We have commented earlier on the Discobolus, whose convincingly life-like movement results from the combination of actually successive poses.   We have said that Lysippus, more than any other, was an illusionist, but even from the very beginning, the sculptor who had little understanding of the complex structure of the knee or the abdomen, made it his aim, by giving a different but equally complicated image, to induce in the spectator the same impression as he would experience before the living model.   Plato was not mistaken when he said that art was primarily artifice; but never, so much as in Greek sculpture, was artifice so well concealed, nor so far identified with the utmost impression of Truth in its most vivid and beautiful form.

TRANSLATED BY BARBARA M. BELL

FIRST PRINTED 1961
BY E. DESFOSSÉS-
NÉOGRAVURE, PARIS

PRINTED IN FRANCE